NERO SU BIANCO

NERO SU BIANCO

Mark Robbins
Robert Storr
Peter Benson Miller
Lyle Ashton Harris
Frank M. Snowden, III
Vincenzo Latronico
Armin Linke
Christian Caliandro
Claudia Durastanti
Taiye Selasi

Carrie Mae Weems
Justin Randolph Thompson
Barbara Chase-Riboud
Elisabetta Benassi
Onyedika Chuke
Meleko Mokgosi
Fred Wilson
Theo Eshetu
Alessandro Ceresoli
Bridget Baker
Senam Okudzeto
Stanley Whitney
Terry Adkins
Lorna Simpson
Giuseppe Stampone
Pietro Ruffo
Francesco Arena
Emily Jacir
Broomberg & Chanarin
Invernomuto
Jebila Okongwu
Nari Ward

CONTRIBUTIONS

Mark Robbins   4
Figure | Ground
Robert Storr   10
Blowing in the Wind
Peter Benson Miller   14
Nero su Bianco
Lyle Ashton Harris   34
Interview with Frank M. Snowden, III

Vincenzo Latronico   62
First Person Colonial
with photographs by Armin Linke

Lyle Ashton Harris   88
Appunti per l'Afro-Barocco
Christian Caliandro   98
*African Italian Identity in Italian
Cinema and Literature, 1946-1982*

Claudia Durastanti   120
Black and White (Don't) Make Gray

Taiye Selasi   136
Do Italian Men Love Black Women?

Biographies   156
End matter   164

ARTWORKS

Echoes of Antiquity and Italian History	Carrie Mae Weems	46
	Justin Randolph Thompson	48
	Barbara Chase-Riboud	50
	Elisabetta Benassi	52
	Onyedika Chuke	54
	Meleko Mokgosi	58
	Fred Wilson	60
The Colonial Legacy	Theo Eshetu	72
	Alessandro Ceresoli	76
	Bridget Baker	80
	Senam Okudzeto	84
African Americans and Italy	Stanley Whitney	108
	Terry Adkins	110
	Lorna Simpson	112
	Elisabetta Benassi	116
Immigration / Integration	Giuseppe Stampone	126
	Pietro Ruffo	128
	Francesco Arena	132
	Emily Jacir	134
Persistent Stereotypes	Broomberg & Chanarin	140
	Invernomuto	144
	Jebila Okongwu	146
	Lyle Ashton Harris	150
	Nari Ward	154

Mark Robbins
Figure | Ground

Centre of equal daughters, equal sons,
All, all alike endear'd...
America, Walt Whitman

The camera pans eerily across the stillness of the temples of Pæstum set in tall scrub grasses. The foreground reveals makeshift grave markers, as a voiceover announces the progress of Allied forces to recently liberated Naples. This begins the second episode of *Paisan*, the middle film of Roberto Rossellini's great war trilogy. Released in 1946, the year following the last battle of the Allied Invasion in Italy, it was shot in the ash and rubble of war, presenting six stories set along the route of the Italian Campaign from Sicily to the Po Valley.

In the crush of Naples still occupied by the Allied troops we see Joe, an African American soldier, drunk, reeling through the street, spotted by the huddle of boys and young men who make their living on the streets. He is sized up for his street value in cigarettes and boots and is eventually spirited away by one of the youngest boys, who Joe calls Paisan. Here amidst the ruins of collapsed buildings, Joe sings and delivers an animated monologue to the uncomprehending, smiling boy about his anticipated return home. The boy seems happy to have a friend, though the soldier still doubles as his quarry. Joe shouts that when he ships out he will enter New York City a hero in a celebration just for him and then take the train home for another celebration. As he says this, his bravado and smile fade as he thinks about what awaits him, and

he repeats twice, "I don't want to go home," before passing out, and presumably having his boots stolen. When we encounter Joe next, he is wearing the uniform of an MP and driving a jeep. He pursues and catches a boy for stealing, eventually recognizing the boy as Paisan, the thief of his own shoes. As Joe berates the child for stealing, he finally switches from English to Italian and so prompts another revelation: that the boy is an orphan whose parents were killed in the bombing. When he takes Paisan "home" to the makeshift sheds where he lives with other orphans, Joe

drops the pair of boots and drives off.

Fifteen minutes in length and essentially a two-character short subject, this brief film segment is both a social document and an artful piece of filmmaking by Rossellini with its own political history. In the context of the exhibition *Nero su Bianco* at the American Academy in Rome, the role of the black male lead stands out. Joe's monologue reflects with Shakespearean depth his inner tension: the soldier liberating Naples is shown to have himself been liberated. He realizes that in going back to America he will lose the rank and position, as well as the relatively equal footing, that the war effort has afforded him, that he may become invisible or be seen as something other than he knows himself to be. In addition, he comes to recognize the boy he calls Paisan as equally displaced and vulnerable. Joe presents a less stereotyped and more complex voice for a black male character than would be seen in a mainstream film distributed by the Hollywood studio system for years.

Rossellini's film is also a reminder of how exposure to different people and places — an essential part of the Academy experience — can have an impact on an individual's own sense of identity. And in its evocation of the immediate postwar period, it helps recall how the mixing of races and classes of servicemen during the war years had a significant effect on social consciousness in the United States.

It is within the postwar period that we can also situate a transformation in the character of the American Academy in Rome and a new openness to diversity both among the Fellows and in their practices and projects. The leadership of Laurance Roberts — an Asianist and museum director who was Director of the Academy between 1947 and 1959 — and his wife, Isabel Spaulding, was instrumental in initiating the institution's more cosmopolitan and international, modern stance. Since its founding in

1894, a time of gilded age affluence but also of social and intellectual upheaval, the Academy had sought to reinforce the classical canon and the belief in classicism. During Roberts' tenure, the Academy instead strived to reconnect with contemporary art practice, and so with the increasing dominance of modernism within schools of art and architecture.

Once artists and architects at the Academy were expected to work together to produce intricate Beaux-

Arts proposals in the so-called Collaborative Problem, a model borrowed from the French Academy and its Prix de Rome. Beginning in 1947, they were free to work in an unsupervised and independent way, choosing topics and forms that best suited their artistic intentions. The rigor of training intersected with personal expression, in figurative, abstract, and conceptual work by artists who were no longer exclusively white males. The first African

American Fellows came to the Academy at mid-century: composer Ulysses Kay in 1949 and sculptor John Walter Rhoden arriving in 1951 as a Fulbright fellow and in residence at the Academy along with classicist Philip Wooby from 1952 to 1954. Writer Ralph Ellison was at the Academy for a two-year Fellowship in 1955–57 (although he reportedly "resist[ed] the allure of the city"). Artist Barbara Chase-Riboud, whose work is in the *Nero su Bianco* exhibition, came in 1957 as an affiliated Fellow through the John Hay Whitney Foundation and became the first woman of color in the School of Fine Arts. (Unlike the School of Classical Studies, which had been coeducational since its inception, the Academy's School of Fine Arts only began to admit women in 1947, with sculptor Concetta Scaravaglione winning the Rome Prize that year.)

In subsequent decades, artists at the Academy have expanded the categories in which they work far beyond the original parameters of their disciplines, often raising questions about art itself and about issues of identity in terms of race, class, ethnicity, and gender. Projects by artists, architects, and scholars have upended conventional readings of history and social narratives. The Academy as an institution has sought to embrace increased openness towards Italy, as well as towards new and changing trends in the arts and historiography.

It was with all this in mind that the discussions leading to *Nero su Bianco* began last spring over lunch with artist Lyle Ashton Harris (FAAR '01 and AAR Trustee). We talked about an exhibition that could look at the legacy of African American artists and scholars at the American Academy. The idea was to tell our institutional history while also reflecting on fundamental relationships between and among the United States, Rome and Italy, and Africa. We discussed ways in which the history and current life of Rome and Italy might be projected and how we might reveal and convey a more complex understanding of the myths and realities of the Academy itself. Another set of conversations last summer with artist, curator, and scholar Robert Storr (AAR Trustee) and with Peter Benson Miller, the Academy's Andrew Heiskell Arts Director, refined our ideas and resulted in the exhibition documented in this volume, for which the three served as co-curators.

The title of the exhibition, *Nero su Bianco*, suggests not only proof — seeing something in black and white — but also the importance of point of view, which yields a particular perspective. Thinking about displacement — of the American soldier in Naples in *Paisan*, of the American artist in Rome — reminds us of how things and the relationships of things can support multiple, often contradictory meanings. What is dominant and what is marginal, what is the thing you see and what is the base or ground against which you see it — are not fixed and immutable relationships. Consider the figure/ground reversal famously shown in Danish psychologist Edgar Rubin's diagram of a vase and two faces. In one reading, the "vase" is privileged and the rest of the image is "background"; in the other, the "background" becomes the dominant figure of two "faces" while the "vase" becomes the space separating them. Looking at the diagram demonstrates the perceptual difficulty of accommodating the two readings simultaneously. Instead

Carrie Mae Weems, *When and Where I Enter*, 2006
Digital C-print, 180×158 cm
Courtesy of the Artist and Jack Shainman Gallery, New York

the mind oscillates between them, revealing both the inherent instability of any perceived relationship and the potential for multiple readings.

That is, perhaps, what a show like this can begin to highlight. There is no single way of approaching issues of identity, as it is inherently a plural condition, which can change or fluctuate over time or according to perspective. As individuals, we are mixed in experience and consciousness and practice affiliations and disaffiliations with varying degrees of fluidity. Freedom comes in the ability to exercise individual choices at each juncture. The power we see in the works in this exhibition comes from the multiplicity of the shifting identities that produced them. Together the artists help us situate art and its aspirations among the complex realities of race and simply what it means to live in America or Europe. They leave us with a richer field of understanding and many open questions.

As is often the case in our work at the Academy, this project required the support of our entire community. A special thanks to the co-curators — Lyle Ashton Harris, Robert Storr, and Peter Benson Miller. Their commitment made this incisive exhibition possible. We are also grateful to the Syde Hurdus Foundation and Miyoung Lee and Neil Simpkins for their support of the exhibition, as well as the Depart Foundation for sponsoring this catalogue. Many of the artists in the exhibition are Residents or Fellows or have been Academy guests; their work is a testament to the Academy's rich and profound legacy, and we deeply appreciate their participation. Current Fellow Denise Rae Costanzo's project on the academies in Rome and national identity ("Eternal City, New Lessons: Modern Architects and Postwar Rome") and forthcoming article ("'A Truly Liberal Orientation': Laurance Roberts, Modern Architecture and the Postwar American Academy in Rome") were both instructive in thinking about the exhibition. Resident Fikret Yegül's early history of the Academy, *Gentlemen of Instinct and Breeding*, was a useful and engaging source. Bill Horrigan and Ann Bremner offered thoughtful readings of the text. Thank you to Lexi Eberspacher and Matteo Ventricelli at the Academy for coordinating the exhibition, and to the following staff for their assistance with research and review of drafts: Sebastian Hierl, Cristina Puglisi, Lavinia Ciuffa, Christine Begley, Shawn Miller, and Marques McClary.

Robert Storr
Blowing in the Wind

Shortly before the turn of the second half of the twentieth century — in 1947 to be exact — and just as the process of de-colonialization was set in motion — often violently by the repression of efforts by colonized people to follow-up on the liberation of Europe from Fascism for which African soldiers had fought and died, the 1945 massacre by white settlers of Algerians demonstrating for freedom from French rule in the town of Sétif being the most notorious example — a Senegalese professor of philosophy founded the publishing house and journal *Présences Africaine*. Both still exist, and it is to his efforts and those of his widow that we owe our familiarity with dozens of novelists, poets, and essayists from the "Dark Continent" and its Diaspora. Chief among them was and is Aimé Césaire, the Martinican poet whose *Cahier d'un retour au pays natal* (*Notebook of a Return to the Native Land*) remains one of the seminal works of the literature of "Negritude," a term that Césaire himself coined, elaborated upon and propagated, as well as the long anti-colonial struggle in all its complex dimensions, those that occurred first of all in the hearts and minds of the colonized men and women.

Although this is a show about the cultural dialectic of "black and white" in Italy, the apparent paradox that the examples mentioned so far are French rather than Italian is owed to the fact that Italy's attempts to fulfill a long standing ambition to carve out colonies

in Africa (as the British, Dutch, Spanish, Portuguese and French had done) were largely confined to the period after the end of World War I, with the subsequent collapse of the Ottoman Empire in 1918, and to the years of Mussolini's imperial adventures in Ethiopia and Libya following the Fascist rise to power in 1922.

The short-lived Italian Empire ended with the Duce's fall in 1943. That same year the Allied troops landed in Sicily and began fighting their way up the boot of Italy to liberate Rome in 1944. The only African American unit to see combat in World War II, the 92nd Division of the Fifth Army, was among them. Their

11

seeming anomalous participation in an Allied campaign in the overwhelmingly white onslaught of British and Americans soldiers inspired Neorealism film director Roberto Rossellini to feature a black G.I. — Joe — in his account of the war's end in *Paisan* (1946).

To use the language of Alouine Diop, Joe was a *"présence africaine."* This presence is everywhere in Italy, indeed everywhere in Europe, and, so it has been since antiquity. From the invasion of the Roman Empire by Hannibal (whose hybrid African and Phoenician heritage is indicative of the ethnic and cultural mixing of the Empire), to his defeat in Carthage (a Phoenician settlement located in what is now Tunisia to which Hannibal was forced to return), and then on to the boat people flocking to Tunisia today hoping for safe passage across the Mediterranean towards safe haven and a new more prosperous life in Europe (although only few actually achieve that goal, while many drown while traveling in the unseaworthy ships of human traffickers or eventually end up in a legal limbo filed as undocumented or stateless immigrants once they make port), we are reminded of the essential truths of Fernand Braudel's scholarly method. The latter in fact set aside the historiography of "great men" and "great nations" in favor of the study of mobile, marbled populations in an ever-changing environment with natural boundaries and regions — the entire Mediterranean basin being the focus of Braudel's paradigmatic inquiry — devoid of any "natural" identities.

Moreover, starting with Josephine Baker and Bricktop in Paris in the Twenties — in painting we could go further back to Henry Ossawa Tanner who exhibited at the Paris Salon in 1896 —, on through the jazz musicians who traveled to Rome in the Fifties and Sixties whose photos still cover the corridor walls of the recording archives at Cinecittà, not to mention writers such as Richard Wright, James Baldwin and Ralph Ellison, who spent two years in Rome, part of that period as a fellow of the American Academy, African Americans have found a place to cultivate their talents in Europe that was often denied them at home in the United States.

Among the most eloquent, albeit eloquently silent, testimonies to this perpetual movement of individuals, groups and cultural wealth with origins in Africa and its Diaspora throughout Italy and the rest of Europe was a work created at the American Academy in Rome by David Hammons in 1993. It consisted of a tribal mask of the tourist trade variety that can be found on sale in markets and airports in Dakar, Venice, New York or London, a mask whose lips quietly "whispered" a steady stream of sand, sand like that which blows across the Mediterranean to the Eternal City, by steady winds off the Sahara. This exhibition consists of other such murmurs. And, sometimes of exclamations of rage and shouts of joy.

Peter Benson Miller
Nero su Bianco

A tall solitary man dressed in black — African American artist Terry Adkins, a former fellow at the American Academy in Rome — stands, whistling, slowly enveloped by clouds of smoke; his figure fades to a barely visible silhouette and then disappears altogether. The sorrowful tune sounds familiar, suggesting a phrase from a hymn or a spiritual, but it eludes our efforts to pin it down. In this way, Lorna Simpson's video installation, *Cloudscape*, offers what Okwui Enwezor has called "a potent symbol of transcendence and grace."[1] Its play of alternating presence and absence, - a formidable if vulnerable self and its erasure, but not without the promise of redemption - sets up many of the themes central to the exhibition *Nero su Bianco*, which considers African American and African Italian identity, subjectivity and agency in contemporary Italy, while highlighting work done by several artists during their time at the American Academy. As the clouds slowly surround Adkins, figure and ground are reversed in a manner not dissimilar to the maneuver discussed by Mark Robbins in his foreword, setting up the state of flux inherent to that relationship and the multiplicity of readings co-existing in this exhibition.

Stark contrasts between black and white in *Cloudscape* give way to shadows and billowing, evanescent vapor, *sfumature* that render firm contours hazy, recalling in the process characteristic elements of Italian culture and its tendency towards obfuscation, trademarks of film noir, as well as the dramatic chiaroscuro techniques of baroque painting and Italian cinema. As it happens, Italian cinema in the years after World War II also offered several talented African American actors, including Harold Bradley and Woody Strode, prominent roles

in the films produced at Cinecittà, the so-called Hollywood on the Tiber.[2] While they were all too often typecast, these actors possessed an agency unheard of in the United States in the same period. In addition to his acting career, Bradley served as a conduit both for trends in music imported from the United States disseminated through his Folkstudio, and ideas central to the Civil Rights movement; Strode was a protagonist in many of the police dramas popular in Italy in the 1980s. More recently, a new generation of actors, in this case second generation African Italians, such as Fred Kuwornu, who was born in Bologna in 1971 to an Italian mother and a Ghanaian father (a surgeon who has lived for over forty years in Italy), have gained a certain prominence onscreen. Kuwornu was cast in Spike Lee's *Miracle at St. Anna* (2008), which retraced the experience of African American soldiers who made up the 92nd division during the Allied invasion of Italy. Despite the visibility afforded by Lee's film, Kuwornu and others like him, including those working in cinema and television in Italy, continue to find themselves in social and political limbo as second-rate citizens.[3]

While he is slowly shrouded in a mysterious fog, which tends to veil his identity, Adkins in Simpson's haunting film nonetheless evokes the free agency of seminal figures like Bradley and Strode looming large in Italian popular culture. As Frank M. Snowden III, suggests in the conversation with Lyle Ashton Harris transcribed in these pages, many African Americans, including distinguished intellectuals such as his father, Frank M. Snowden Jr., felt much more liberated and welcomed in Italy than they did in the United States. He notes the irony of "African American soldiers [who] returned from fighting abroad to destroy Nazism and racism only to rediscover [on their return to the United States] that they were compelled to endure conditions that were unworthy of a civilized na-

tion." Thus, despite a very different, but similarly vexed history of race relations shaped by Mussolini's racial laws and the colonial enterprise in Africa, postwar Italy offered a refuge for many African Americans, a respite from the relentless racism they suffered on the other side of the Atlantic.

This was certainly the case for William Demby, an African American writer and perceptive art critic who first came to Italy with the Allied armed forces during World War II. In an article published in 1996, he described himself as "a gentle cultured version of those thousands of boisterous American Negro troops who had suddenly appeared in the landscape of war and just as suddenly disappeared having taught the Italians to boogie-woogie." He notes that many Italians "assumed that he was a fashionable victim of American racism but that [he] was also living in political asylum."[4] He later explained his reasons for choosing Rome: "the smart-ass urban sophistication of Paris never appealed to me." Rather, he sought "the gritty life of the pure artist" in Rome.[5] Whatever his reasons for remaining in Italy, much of his writing contended with the theme of personal subjectivity and the condition of an African American intellectual in an international context. An expatriate living in Rome for much of his career, he made the theme of the insider/outsider central to his work. Demby's fascinating career as a writer, journalist and critic touched on a wide range of intellectual pursuits and thus provides unparalleled insight into the status of an African American in Italian cultural circles.

Arriving in Naples in 1943 with a unit of the United States Fifth Army led by Lieutenant General Mark Clark, Demby was photographed with his brother, Frank, in Rome in 1945; both brothers returned to the United States after the war and graduated from Fisk University, in Nashville. His studies completed, William Demby traveled back to Italy in 1947, where he wrote much of his first novel, *Beetlecreek*, which was translated into Italian by Fernanda Pivano in 1950. Buoyed by his sudden celebrity and introductions to publisher Alberto Mondadori, and writer Elio Vittorini and poet Eugenio Montale, Demby was commissioned to travel through East Africa with the photographer Marjory Collins for Mondadori's new weekly magazine *Epoca*. The article and accompanying photographs describe the situation in Eritrea, a former Italian colony, nine years after its independence.[6] The experience introduced him to the challenges of navigating the complicated political situation in Cold War Italy. He recalled that "when I returned to Rome, having been the first journalist to interview Haile Selassie and having risked my life flying to Gondar with a drunken American pilot, I discovered that because I had given Lionello Torossi, who had been acting informally as my literary agent, a number of shorter versions of my *Epoca* articles to be published in the communist daily newspaper *Paese Sera*, Mondadori's love affair with the elegant young American novelist had begun to cool."[7] Demby later addressed the effects of the postcolonial situations on race relations in Italy head on in his novel *The Catacombs* (1965). In an interview conducted in 2008, Demby explained the role played by Doris, one of the two main characters, stating that she represented "a stock character in Italian social life, a black goddess, or the black woman who is easily available, the woman who comes from colonialism."[8]

In 1953, Demby married the Italian writer, translator and actress Lucia Drudi, the sister of art critic Gabriella Drudi, the wife of painter Toti Scialoja. The interracial union made waves and introduced him further into the top echelons of the Italian literary and artistic avant-garde. Prior to his marriage, Demby lived in Via San Teodoro in Rome in a sort of artist's commune with Marcello Muccini and artist Renzo Vespignani. Gaspero Del Corso, who, with Irene Brin, ran the Galleria dell'Obelisco, dubbed them the *Gruppo Portonaccio*, after the bleak quarter "with its funereal high-rise housing developments," which, Demby noted, served as "the political landscape of almost every neo-realistic film." The film world was one he knew well; he regularly frequented the weekly meetings of the cinema club at the Cinema Bernini, an important gathering place for left-leaning intellectuals. It was there that he met the film director Citto Maselli, an associate of Michelangelo Antonioni. Fluent in Italian, Demby translated Italian screenplays and subtitles into English, working for such directors as Federico Fellini; he also served as assistant director for dialogues in Roberto Rossellini's film *Europa 51*. He later befriended artists Mimmo Rotella, Tano Festa, Francesco Lo Savio and Mario Schifano, writing on several occasions about their work. In one particularly striking episode, Demby was called by the producers of the Italian television program *Il Signore delle 21* to introduce Louis Armstrong and Ella Fitzgerald, who performed live on the air. The program was a crucial avenue through which a broad Italian public was introduced to American jazz music. Impressed by the fact that he was a cousin of Benny Carter, a legend among African American musicians, Armstrong and Fitzgerald perceived Demby as "an early example of the Civil Rights revolution having transformed the racial situation in Italy."[9]

This exhibition attempts to take stock of the degree to which the state of affairs with regard to race in Italy has changed over the course of the second half of the twentieth century. Many feel that Demby's optimism may have been premature. The title *Nero su Bianco* evokes not only the subtle tonal contrasts of Simpson's video, which blur the distinctions upon which racial identity has long been predicated, and the fairly exceptional case of William Demby, who forged an important writing career as an African American in a predominately white Italy. It also calls for a plurality of perspectives in a free and open dialogue. In Italian, the expression *nero su bianco* usually refers to the printed word on the pages of a book or a daily newspaper, suggesting something that is documented, proven or worthy of note. Rendered official in black and white, the enunciation of facts or the airing of opinions in a public forum endows them with authority and engenders debate and discussion. Putting something in *nero su bianco* entails taking a public position on an issue, which is all too rare in a country where powers lurking in the shadows continue to hold sway. On the one hand, this project attempts to take just such a stand and in so doing initiate an ongoing debate, providing a forum for a host of artists to express their views on many of the issues related to the question of identity in Italy today. The phrase *nero su bianco* also suggests legal procedures — contracts, official documents, legislation, identity cards, residence permits — that make up the bureaucratic apparatus defining and patrolling identity, distinguishing who gets to be Italian from who does not. Many of the works in this exhibition explore and question not only the radical demographic shifts and attitudes affecting the country, but also the factors that determine the status and rights, or lack of them, of Italy's non-white populations and the recent immigrants arriving with increasing frequency on its shores.

An overview and assessment of the past several decades, *Nero su Bianco* features work by an international group of artists — many of them closely affiliated with the American Academy in Rome — as a means for taking the cultural, social and political temperature in Italy today. With that goal and within that overall range, the exhibition examines and questions key sites, paying special attention to their historical origins and legacies and the conditions and modes of production that shaped them. It embraces an ambitious scope of inquiry and methodologies by emphasizing research and developing conceptual projects in a variety of media including film, sculpture, painting, installation, photography and performance. As it has been for over two millennia, contemporary Italy is a uniquely rich site for inquiry. From ancient Rome to the present, migration, trade, slavery, and imperial conquest have formed the demographic panoply of the peninsula and its discourse of racial identity and belonging. Located at the crossroads of Europe and Africa,

Italy receives waves of immigrants that continue to arrive daily on the southern coasts as, to varying degrees, they have for centuries. The most recent influx has opened a space to address the urgent and profound demographic shifts reshaping nationhood in Italy and European society more broadly. Oddly, however, an open public discussion of the complex issues related to Italy's colonial period and its current role as magnet for African populations fleeing political turmoil is largely lacking in Italy beyond the populist slogans of a certain kind of predictable electioneering discourse. As Vincenzo Latronico notes in these pages, "Italians never speak of colonialism; they don't study it in school, they don't remember it on special dates and occasions, they do not reconstruct it through monuments and museums."

To be sure, the Americas have a complex and profoundly troubled history of race relations of their own, generating tensions that have by no means been entirely resolved, even in the so-called "post-race" era. Grappling with this heritage and its many sources of ambiguity and ambivalence has produced a hyper awareness of ethnic and cultural difference that sets the tone for productive intercultural exchange. In that spirit, this exhibition proposes to convene and connect a series of conversations animated by recurring echoes of the American experience, one that, as the examples cited above demonstrate, has been inescapably intertwined with Italy since the end of World War II. The project seeks furthermore to open a space for critical dialogue engaging the larger issues raised by our increasingly interlaced, but not always cosmopolitan realities and their impact on Europe's fitful evolution and its perplexingly simultaneous integration and disintegration.

The American Academy in Rome has long played host to artists who subvert and problematize conventional narratives and histories. Accordingly, it is a fitting venue for an international survey encompassing multiple perspectives on seismic shifts in private as well as public perceptions of identity, particularly regarding subjectivity and agency within the African American, European and African spheres and the overlap between them. The exhibition is animated by this self-conscious institutional critique; questions raised here call for a fundamental reconsideration of the historical idea of the Academy, underscoring the need to recast "the canon" and reposition the institution as a forum for open discussion and constructive debate about ethnic and cultural hybridity in the world generally, in Europe particularly and even more specifically in Italy. Taking advantage of the intellectual and creative community at the Academy, the project benefits from collaborations between visual artists and scholars fostering a series of conversations in an interdisciplinary framework engaging the increasingly specific and multi-centered issues discussed in detail here below while sustaining a critical dialogue.

Echoes of Antiquity and Italian History

Several works in *Nero su Bianco* hark back to antiquity in order to unpack how difference has been inscribed in classical literature, Roman art and history and the foundational myths of Rome itself. As he was in Simpson's *Cloudscape*, Terry Adkins is the protagonist of Justin Randolph Thompson's *Loquens de Fluminibus (Speaking of Rivers)*, a performance and sound-based Super 8 film shown on a monitor in an altered television console. It draws upon an interview conducted with Adkins at the American Academy in Rome in 2010 in which Adkins discusses an unrealized project based on the Roman comic playwrights Plautus and Terence and a meditation upon artistic figuration as servitude. The title combines the one Adkins gave to his Roman works, *Flumen Orationis*, Latin for "River of Speech," with Langston Hughes' reflection on legacy in *The Negro Speaks of Rivers*. Thompson's work features a monologue by Adkins decrying the institutional propagation of the black image and illuminating the challenges that face a younger generation of black artists. Shot inside a neoclassical theatre, the film draws upon the subject of servitude as addressed by Plautus and Terence and the notion of the volatility of socially prescribed roles. Reflecting on an intergenerational discourse that passes from figuration to abstraction and from words to sound, the piece explores the Italian context as a historic site for the mobilization of creative forms and fluid identities.

In Carrie Mae Weems' *The Edge of Time*, one of the photographs from her *Roaming* series, a specter in a long black dress stands in front of a dramatic, sunbleached urban panorama. The site is Matera, in Basilicata, which stands in for the faded grandeur of any number of formerly great cities on the Italian peninsula. For many artists — including photographers such as Henri Cartier-Bresson and Marjory Collins, as well as the painter and writer Carlo Levi, who immortalized the city in his memoir, *Christ*

Stopped at Eboli — Matera, a warren of subterranean churches and cave-like dwellings, was virtually synonymous with a primitive way of life, the survival of ancient superstition and a peasant culture cut off temporally and physically from the modern world. The phantom presence in Weems' photograph is thus quite literally hovering on the edge of time. She is brought further into relief as a witness by the apparently desolate architecture with its empty windows, an insalubrious conglomeration of houses abandoned by its inhabitants. They were removed to a new town on the outskirts of Matera in the late 1950s in a controversial social experiment designed to ameliorate their living conditions. For this reason, however, Matera offers a fitting setting for Weems' project. The artist has discussed the *Roaming* series as an attempt to challenge the way architecture, even sublimely decayed and poetic cityscapes like Matera, enforces the relationship of power between the state and its subjects. In a sequence of performances, such as the one captured in *The Edge of Time*, Weems used her own body to lead the viewer into that relationship, questioning it in the process. In so doing, she acts like Dante's Virgil in a black dress, a guide hovering above and leading us into Matera's empty labyrinth, a maze of streets and troglodyte dwellings structuring the way of life of its residents for thousands of years.

Consistent with interests that she developed during a fellowship at the American Academy in Rome in 1958, when she made her first sculptures in bronze, Barbara Chase-Riboud conjures up in *Cleopatra's Bed* the powerful political agency and erotic allure of the legendary Queen of Egypt who took on Rome. It evokes a passage from Plutarch's first-century description of Cleopatra standing beneath "a canopy of gold" as she dazzled the Roman general Mark Antony "with many chandeliers lighted at once in patterns of squares." The artist confirmed that "the genesis of my interest in Cleopatra is based on my fascination with power as wielded by women throughout the ages." Small cast bronze tiles are linked to form a chain mail drapery covering a chaise-longue. Each tessera in the supple, fabric-like mosaic bears an incised or relief pattern composed of the artist's own invented hieroglyphics. The work is clearly informed by Chase-Riboud's long-standing interest in Egyptian art forms, which she discovered on a trip to Egypt during her year in Italy, the first African American woman to stay for an extended period at the Academy.

Other works revisit sea voyages from classical literature and myth, underlining the role played by the Mediterranean as a conduit for trade and migration and the site of decisive naval battles, such as Actium, which sealed Cleopatra's fate. Elisabetta Benassi's video *Capo Portiere Bonjour* documents the arrival of a clandestine shipment of African immigrants in a battered fishing vessel on the shores south of Rome near Latina. Its human cargo dispersed, the abandoned boat with its engines still running and its painted metal prow lists in the surf lapped by gentle, but incessant waves as dawn slowly breaks. Benassi's work derives its power from the fact that illicit crossings from North Africa to Lampedusa and other points on the Italian coast reenact the epic sea voyages undertaken by Odysseus and Æneas in the aftermath of the Trojan War. Confronted with this makeshift craft, we are reminded of the real hardships suffered by those mythological travelers. Like contemporary Africans fleeing civil wars and political persecution, Greek warriors returning home after many years away or setting out for unchartered territory had to contend with violent seas, starvation, pirates, overcrowded conditions and other formidable adversities.

Requisitioned boats, of course, were also central to Marcus Garvey's crusade to return former slaves to Africa via his Black Star Line. Born in Jamaica, Garvey, a political leader and entrepreneur, was a staunch proponent of Black Nationalism and the Pan-African movement. The Black Star Line venture was an attempt to redress, even though it could by no means eradicate, the memory of the horrific conditions endured by Africans sent to the Americas by Atlantic slave traders. The banner hanging from the façade of the McKim, Mead & White Building, another work by Benassi, is emblazoned with Garvey's slogan "Ships and Still More Ships." Conflating all of these voyages, Benassi's image of a single boat with its rusting hull against a marine landscape featuring Monte Circeo in the background — a site suffused with antiquity — demythologizes Virgil's heroic account of Rome's origins in the *Æneid*. Instead of a determined band of warriors destined to be the masters of the Mediterranean, we imagine a group of desperate, half-starved refugees staggering ashore unsure of what awaits them in a hostile land, not unlike the waves of African immigrants that continue to arrive in search of political asylum and a better life. Not long after Benassi shot this video, the boat was dislodged from the sand and seized by Italian authorities. Some of the passengers were rounded up and brought to temporary shelters; others claimed political protection, while still others escaped to freedom.

Onyedika Chuke also disrupts traditional narratives from the classical past and its construction of the foreign other in his *The Untitled: 1919*, in which he dismantles and recomposes a cast of a Roman sculpture. As defined by Sigmund Freud in his analysis of the Uncanny (*unheimliche*), the term describes something that is both familiar and oddly unfamiliar at once. Chuke notes that the year 1919 marked the publication of Freud's influential text, which was to have a profound impact on the understanding of the individual in modern society, as well as the birth of Mikhail Kalashnikov — the inventor of the AK-47 — and the printing of Benito Mussolini's "Fascist Manifesto." In the same year, Fascists attacked the office of the Socialist newspaper *Avanti!* and the Italian government expanded its sphere of control in the African colony of Libya. In all of these cases, according to the artist, delineations of boundaries in both a physical and intellectual sense — whether through violence, intimidation, colonialism or the printed word — contributed to contemporary ideas about race, immigration and identity.

Evolving notions of race in contemporary Italy are also reflected, and sometimes checked, in a wide array of decorative arts and monuments; works in *Nero su Bianco* engage the multiplicity of these artefacts and experiences in a variety of ways. Projects focus on how race, subjectivity and agency are often embodied in and enforced by material culture, not only the Roman and Hellenistic sculptures altered by Chuke, but also historical objects tied to subsequent periods in Italian history, such as heraldic coats of arms and Venetian mirrors. In *Terra Pericolosa II*, a large installation of drawings, Meleko Mokgosi unpacks the legacy of Italian *imprese* and their continuing currency in Africa. He investigates notions of inclusion and exclusion at the level of the nation-state, scrutinizing the politics of identity inscribed in the coat of arms adopted by his country of origin, Botswana, in 1966, the year it achieved independence, and the specific imagery employed to construct selfhood under a national banner. In so doing, he recognizes in the peculiar language, layout and design of the coat of arms an unconventional narrative form, but one that is no less effective in sanctioning certain key aspects of the nation-state. The emblems themselves derive from a specifically local African context commemorating struggle and independence: a traditional African shield, the zebra, a sign of Botswana's abundant wildlife, sorghum, a staple crop, and three cogwheels that represent industry. But they are nonetheless harnessed to a visual system imported from Europe, converting the concise declaration of lineage and prestige central to aristocratic power into a means of constructing national identity that remains profoundly shaped by colonialism.

Another artist interested in the symbols embraced by African nations since they achieved independence from colonial rule — most notably in a series entitled *Flags* (2009) — Fred Wilson, in the work in this exhibition, reworks one of the hallmarks of Venetian culture.

Taking as his point of departure the large mirrors made in Murano for patrician palaces, he translates their rococo flourishes and etched motifs into smoky black glass. The title, *Emilia's Mirror, Act 2, Scene 5*, refers to the climactic scene in Shakespeare's *Othello* when the Moor, enraged by irrational jealousy, smothers Desdemona in her bed. The darkness of the mirror recalls the biblical passage from 1 Corinthians: "For now we see through a glass, darkly; but then face to face: now I know in part; but then shall I know even as also I am known." For centuries, murky mirrors offered only partial likenesses; as a result they were often invoked as metaphors for shadowy sight and poor reflections. Wilson also refers both to the omnipresence of Africans in cosmopolitan Venetian society and to their representation in fine and decorative arts, where they are often overlooked or taken for granted, and the question of Othello's identity — defined as much by the color of his skin as his accomplishments as a leader — in Shakespeare's tragedy. Mirrors shape perceptions of individual identity, something denied to Othello, who is forced to renounce his own name and is cast back into anonymity at the end of the play. The black glass in Wilson's work and its opacity, which refuses either mimesis or self-recognition, suggests this oscillation between selfhood and its erasure, even as the rich hue Africanizes a typically Venetian cultural artifact and conflates figure and ground.

Representing the United States at the 2003 Venice Biennale, Wilson presented *Speak of Me as I Am*, a title echoing Othello's final plea. It also used black Murano glass in a monumental chandelier, part of an elaborate installation that harnessed museological display as a medium to question assumptions about race, identity and history. Wilson's dark mirror also reminds us of Michael E. Nowlin's defense of the critic Lionel Trilling's notion of an "adversary" or subversive intention characterizing modern writing, and creative expression more generally, against charges leveled by Cornel West, among others, that Trilling was a mandarin apologist for high culture. In *Beyond Culture* (1965), Trilling had defined "adversary culture" as having a clear intention to "detach the reader from the habits of thought and feeling that the larger culture imposes, of giving him a ground and a vantage point from which to judge and condemn, and perhaps revise, the culture that produced him." Nowlin, in turn, argued that "adversary culture" was "essentially the dark mirror image of a frustrated humanistic enterprise."[10] Similarly, *Emilia's Mirror* explores the blind spots in the Western scholarly tradition and contemporary society as a whole.

The Colonial Legacy

Mussolini's invasion of Abyssinia in 1935, and Italy's short-lived African Empire, more generally, brought questions of racial identity in Italy into sharp focus. Indeed, the cosmopolitanism that characterized Venice from the Renaissance onwards was largely ignored after unification in 1871. Generally speaking, a constructed national identity was harnessed to notions of racial purity that depended on a stark contrast between black and white, a means to assert "whiteness" as a prerequisite of *italianità*. Italian racial identity, in contrast to the operations of national fantasies in other European countries, was not linked to an autoreferential myth, but hinged upon the definition of a diametrically opposed other.[11] This trend gathered force and culminated in colonial legislation in 1936-37 governing racial relations. Several works in *Nero su Bianco* revisit this period and its aftermath. Despite the fact that Eritrea achieved independence from Italy in 1947, the physical traces of the colonial period remain evident; just as they attempted to construct hierarchies of race based upon skin color, Italian colonizers radically transformed African cities under their control. One of these, Asmara, attracted Alessandro Ceresoli, who lived and worked in the city for an extended period. There, he created a series of works in collaboration with Eritrean artisans at a local glassworks. The results are prototypes in glass that recall the characteristic design of Italian modernist architecture of the colonial period, such as the "Fiat Tagliero," a service station built by futurist architect Giuseppe Pettazzi in Asmara in 1938. In reworking Pettazzi's design and creating a line of household furniture in collaboration with local craftsmen, Ceresoli created hybrid objects that endowed active agency to a population denied such power under colonial rule and the current autocratic regime in Eritrea. At the same time, by domesticating Pettazzi's colonial relic and bringing it into a household sphere, he calls attention to and critically scrutinizes a period and an idiosyncratic patrimony that has been virtually erased from Italian collective memory.

If Ceresoli takes on structures built by Italian colonizers in Africa and their role in shaping a kind of hybrid subjectivity, Theo Eshetu interrogates the implications of a monument expropriated from Africa as part of Mussolini's efforts to herald a modern Roman empire. In 1935, the Axum Obelisk, a twenty-five meter tall, 160 ton stele, believed to have been built in the third century, was transported to Rome as a war trophy and installed in front of the then Ministry for the Colonies. The feat was intended to echo the triumphs of Roman Emperors, who erected granite obelisks from Egypt as focal points for their building campaigns as symbols of imperial dominance. After the capitulation of Mussolini, the building was given to the United Nations and transformed into the Food Agricultural Organization. In this revised context, the Axum Obelisk came to represent FAO's mission and Ethiopia as a focal point for international aid without, however, shedding its post-colonial connotations. The conversion from a marker of colonial subjugation to one of postwar cooperation did not convince everyone. For Ethiopians in Rome and the Orthodox Church, it was an important presence in the Eternal City, evidencing a spiritual tie between Rome and Axum as two important capitals of Christianity. There were others who argued that the obelisk should be returned to its original site as a gesture of reconciliation. A virulent debate continued for several decades until 2002 when the stele was struck by lightning and subsequently dismantled; it was repatriated to Ethiopia in 2008 and reassembled in Axum, an unprecedented engineering feat greeted with joyous celebration. Theo Eshetu's fifteen monitor video installation, which draws upon narrative and compositional forms typical of traditional Ethiopian painting, documents the whole process as a "ritual ceremony of transformation." Despite the fact that Eshetu's work is intimately tied to Rome, its appearance in *Nero su Bianco* is the first time that it has been shown in the Italian capital.

Another lightning rod for complicated postcolonial attitudes was Franco Prosperi and Gualtiero Jacopetti's *Africa Addio*, a sensationalized "shockumentary" about the end of colonial regimes in Africa that incorporated footage of the Zanzibar revolution. It was a resounding success with the Italian public when it was first screened in Rome in 1966, but there were allegations of inauthenticity, including the accusation that the co-directors staged the scene of the execution of a Congolese Simba rebel. Jacopetti was arrested on charges of murder, but later released when the filmmakers produced proof that they had arrived just before the actual execution took place. As part of an ongoing project, South African artist Bridget Baker explores the complex reception of that film, including a mock trial and debate sponsored by *La Tribuna Illustrata* and broadcast on the weekly *Cordialmente* State television program, in which a jury of twenty-three newspaper editors selected from Roman high schools were convened to determine if the filmmakers were guilty of racism. Among the charges was the accusation that the directors used different camera lenses to make African characters seem less photogenic than their European counterparts. During the proceedings, two witnesses for the prosecution, a Nigerian, Ibe Ekesie, and an Ethiopian, Tesfay Selassie, were questioned at length by the jury. Working with newsreels and footage from the Istituto Luce and the testimony of par-

ticipants, Baker explores the complex dynamics of agency and the multiplicity of empowered voices in colonial and postcolonial narratives.

Overturning many of the tropes of travelogues written by Europeans in Africa, a narrative form that did a great deal to domesticate and colonize overseas territory, Vincenzo Latronico, here represented by a translated excerpt of his book *Narciso nelle colonie. Un altro viaggio in Etiopia*, also questions a conventional vehicle for the western gaze. In the romantic era, in particular, the illustrated travel account was often framed as a personal voyage of discovery in which the author's self emerged in relation to the exotic other. Accompanied by the photographer and filmmaker Armin Linke, who contributed the photographs to the volume, Latronico set out in the early months of 2012 on a three-week trek through Ethiopia; their itinerary was planned with an eye to Latronico's genealogy and his precursors' ties to the colonial enterprise in the horn of Africa. They had intended, for example, to follow the route of the railroad built by Italian engineers, one of whom was Latronico's grandfather. After this proved impossible, which frustrated a straightforward path to a so-called heart of darkness, the author's self-conscious attempts to retrace his family history are interwoven with observations about present day Ethiopia. These tend to upend, rather than endorse, western assumptions about contemporary Africa. Linke's photographs complement Latronico's "archaeology of the present," which acknowledges with every step the partialness of every single perspective. Images alternate between panoramic scenes of vast arid landscapes, which update and gently subvert the pictorial conventions of paintings created by nineteenth-century artists like Eugène Fromentin and Gustave Guillaumet, and unflinching close-up views of contemporary Ethiopia. These include a photograph of the remnants of a Fascist monument in a public park in Addis Ababa, a spiral staircase in which each step represents a year of the colonial occupation. An Ethiopian lion, a symbol favored by Haile Selassie, perches on the top, converting the staircase into an elaborate pedestal.

African Americans and Italy

As we saw with William Demby, the arrival of African American soldiers in the Allied army during World War II helped introduce jazz culture into Italy. By the 1960s, when Louis Armstrong and Ella Fitzgerald performed live on television, jazz had become even more pervasive. Some hint of the musical revolution wrought by this transatlantic import can be heard in the tune whistled by Terry Adkins in *Cloudscape*. The syncopated rhythms of distinctly American sounds resurface in the colorful checkerboard paintings by Stanley Whitney, who has divided his time between New York and Italy for several decades. Drawing upon the solid masonry of ancient Roman walls and the intense light for which the Italian capital is revered by artists, Whitney creates sensual luminous grids of vibrant colors structured by horizontal lines. While he invokes the hues of African textiles, Whitney's paintings also suggest the attempts by modernist predecessors, including Piet Mondrian in paintings such as *Broadway Boogie Woogie* (1942-43), to create visual equivalents for music. In Whitney's paintings, the horizontal lines suggest those of sheet music, creating a formal matrix for the vibrating squares, whose alternating color contrasts create a counterpoint of syncopated rhythm punctuated by sudden riffs. In *Primordial Color II*, each block of color gyrates and pulses within the confines of its own cell like a solo musician in the midst of an improvisational passage surrounded by fellow band members tapping out a constant beat. In his attempt to capture primordial or elemental colors, Whitney demonstrates affinities with the writings of Pier Paolo Pasolini and Alberto Moravia, both of whom, as Christian Caliandro notes in these pages, explored difference and identity in terms of an archaic past shared by Europeans and Africans alike.

The arrival of African American troops in Naples not only ushered in the wide popularity of jazz music, it also marked an important milestone in the Civil Rights movement. While the military remained hierarchical and segregation continued to reign among soldiers, the experience of war began to break down the barriers. Demby stated in his interview: "And racial segregation! There was plenty of it, but I didn't let it get under my skin." He noted that the United States army, mobilized quickly and trained to work in a cohesive unit, nonetheless ended up reflecting the social problems of society at large. Still the war instilled in many African American soldiers the seeds of a collective consciousness. As Demby testified: "Only in the army could black people of all different cultural groupings and backgrounds live together and slowly begin to know each other."[12] Working with discarded tin objects — in this case what appears to be part of an airplane fuselage, the fender of a truck or a gasoline container with parts of a license plate or an inventory number — Terry Adkins, in his work *Greater Deeps (from Firmament RHA),* pays tribute to his father, Robert Hamilton Adkins, who disembarked in Naples with Allied troops in 1943. Roberto Rossellini's *Paisan* immortalized the impact of that experience on one African American soldier. Demby provides another first-person account:

"Suddenly we were landing in Naples, which had just been bombed, and we had our overloaded backpacks strapped on our backs and are struggling to keep our balance on the floating pontoon walkways and try our best to keep from falling into Naples' bay. Everything was destroyed on the outskirts of Naples. I've never seen such wanton destruction, a ghostly landscape of broken buildings. For almost three days and three nights, we inched our way north under almost constant bombardment."[13]

In *Greater Deeps,* as a testament to his father, Adkins has crafted a kind of crucifix out of pockmarked metal, a scarred relic of warfare. It suggests not only the soldier's sacrifice, but also Demby's "ghostly landscape" strewn with the scattered debris left behind by an advancing army. Responding to the artist's Catholic faith, Adkins' miraculous transformation of a humble cast-off into a work of art, an ex-voto to his father, offers a transcendent symbol of the nascent collective consciousness shaped by the war, one soldier at a time.

Immigration / Integration

Italy is currently inundated with a new influx of immigrants from Africa, many of them arriving clandestinely via unregulated and highly dangerous routes by sea from North Africa to various points on the Italian coastline. Even as the opening of this exhibition nears, the crisis has assumed almost biblical proportions. The other day, a fishing boat smuggling human cargo capsized 60 miles (96 km) off the coast of Libya and 120 miles (193 km) south of Lampedusa. The death toll is catastrophic: 700 passengers are missing and feared dead. Over 1,500 migrants have died thus far in 2015, a number that is thirty times higher than last year's equivalent figure. For every immigrant who makes it safely to shore, there are many who perish in the attempt at the hands of unscrupulous human traffickers. Pietro Ruffo, in a series of watercolors entitled *Mar di Sicilia,* uses picturesque seascapes of beaches and cliffs as the backdrop for abstract shapes borrowed from statistical charts documenting the cause of death of countless people attempting to cross into Europe. Beneath the pleasant veneer of the watercolor scenes — reminiscent of those by foreign artists entranced by Italy's unparalleled natural beauty — there lurks a far bleaker and disquieting reality. The sinuous line represents the confines of Europe set by the Treaty of Schengen, which traced an arbitrary boundary in the Mediterranean, effectively binding Italy to a European zone and arbitrarily separating it from North Africa, to which it has been linked culturally and commercially for centuries. If the concentric circles are like Charybdis, treacherous whirlpools sucking desperate travelers to their deaths, then the line in the sea is a modern version of Scylla, rocky shoals allegorized by Homer into a sea monster, which spelled disaster for Odysseus. Both of them guard the coast of Sicily today as their literary counterparts did in antiquity. Ruffo thus underlines the stark contrast between the promise of Italy, here represented by scenes that wouldn't look out of place in a poster advertising Sicily as a tourist playground, and the brutal price paid by those caught between persecution in Africa and Europe's outdated and discriminatory immigration policies.

Giuseppe Stampone, himself the offspring of Italian parents who emigrated to France in search of employment, also contrasts the arduous journey endured by many immigrants, represented in his work by a shipping container placed in the Triangle Garden across the street from the Academy, and the dream of a decent life that many hope awaits them in Europe. Here, too, a modest domestic environment, recreated in Stampone's work by a schematic chalk diagram on blackboard — more of a how-to set for creating a home than an actual lived space — sits uncomfortably within the unforgiving international trade networks conjured up by the container. His work, too, indicts those smugglers that reduce human cargo to the state of expendable merchandise, but ultimately his work is animated by a cautious optimism. For many immigrants, Italy is more of a way-station than a destination; the conversations reverberating inside Stampone's container represent a heterogenous population of migrants as they communicate with each other and with their far-flung family members in Italy and beyond. This matrix of overlapping voices knits Italy into an ever more complex cultural fabric that exceeds the geographical confines of the Italian peninsula.

The Lampedusa crisis has played out dramatically in the Italian press, accompanied by much hand wringing, but little effective action on the part of European and Italian officials. Meanwhile the death toll continues to rise. The distance separating Italy and Africa has taken on increasing importance as news accounts zoom in on the precise sites where boats have overturned in the Mediterranean, measuring in each case the distance of the boat from its point of origin and its intended destination within the geographical expanse dividing Africa from Italy. Francesco Arena's work *Passi* takes these distances as the principal coordinates for a work of art articulated in two parts: a performance and a sculpture. He has measured the expanse of sea separating the island of Lampedusa from the coast of Tunisia, on the one hand, and that from Lampedusa to the Italian mainland, on the other. The artist notes that Lampedusa, while territorially part of Italy, is actually closer to Africa. In an effort to convey the import of these distances geographically and conceptually, Arena has instructed two performers to walk a prescribed route within the Academy, linking the various works in the exhibition in the process. Each performer follows a set path such that at the culmination of the exhibition their combined steps will have covered the distances between Lampedusa and each of the two continents, respectively. Each day that the exhibition is open, they walk 5.11 km and 8.61 km. At the point where the paths of the performers meet, Arena has placed, like a milestone, a sculpture made up of two bars in mirror-polished bronze. The length of the bars corresponds to a single stride taken by the performers. Multiplied by the numbers engraved on the bars, we obtain the distances dividing Lampedusa from each mainland. The work effectively inscribes these distances into the confines of the Academy, bringing Lampedusa into the heart of the exhibition and underscoring the geographical position of Italy at the crossroads of the geopolitical crisis resulting from the massive displacement of African immigrants.

Of course, the efforts to distinguish Italy culturally and geographically from Africa and the Middle East — reversing centuries of cross-cultural exchange effected by migration, trade and conquest, not to mention slavery — downplays many of the explicit examples of that dialogue that can still be seen in Italy today. Emily Jacir's *stazione* is an intervention planned for the 2009 Venice Biennale in which the artist proposed to translate the names of each *vaporetto* stop into Arabic and place them next to their Italian counterparts, creating a bilingual transportation route through the city, from the Lido to Piazzale Roma along the line #1. As Jacir notes in the brochure accompanying her project, evidence of exchange between the Arab world and Venice are clearly evident along the Grand Canal at the various points serviced by the *vaporetto*; forms that migrated from the East can be seen in the architecture of Ca' d'Oro, as well as other structures. Venetian craftsmen emulated the techniques of Arab artisans in bookbinding, metalwork, textiles and glassblowing, inheriting a process invented in Palestine. Venice was also the main European point of entry for Arab science, medicine, cartography and philosophy, and Venetian printing houses translated the works of Averroes and Avicenna, among others. The Arabic translations added to the *vaporetto* route underline Italy's shared heritage with the Arab world. The project reminds us of its deep and varied cultural origins, but it also cautions us about the risks of cutting off Italy from its Mediterranean neighbors and closing its borders to the innovative ideas brought by future immigrants, including those from Arabic speaking countries.

Nero su Bianco also visits key sites, such as Termini, multi-ethnic neighborhoods like Tor Pignattara and the New Esquiline Market in Rome, call centers, and internet points, which, despite the widespread availability of cellular phones, remain everyday catalysts in the development of a new subjectivity. Lyle Ashton Harris, in his *Roman Strangers* series, photographed passersby of various nationalities and hues in Termini, Rome's central railway station. People of indeterminate ethnicity cross paths in one of the capital city's busiest transportation hubs; their trajectory appears as fluid as their unfixed identity. Black and white dissolves in Harris' images into a cosmopolitan reality unacknowledged by Italian mainstream media.

Urban markets have emerged as one of the most visible and contested sites in which immigrants have asserted an active agency in Italian society. Senam Okudzeto's selections from the *Portes-Oranges* series features metal sculptures used by Ghanaian fruit sellers to display their wares. They are accompanied in an installation by approximately one thousand oranges scattered across the gallery floor and a video projection documenting the fruit sellers at work. This project is part of her *Ghana-Must-Go* series, which, according to the artist, explores concepts of "modernity, memory and material culture," using images of contemporary Africa as a point of departure to mark a growing awareness of social complexity. Evoking the marketplace of art and food, she questions the status of the art object in a manner reminiscent of Marcel Duchamp; the metal sculptures, as found objects, have affinities with Duchamp's readymade bottle racks, which the artist removed from their regular context and promoted to the realm of art. The revival of interest in Duchamp and in Dada more generally in the 1960s was largely due to the efforts of an Italian, Arturo Schwarz, who dedicated several exhibitions to Duchamp in his gallery in Milan. Transposed to an Italian context, Okudzeto's work, especially its use of oranges, takes on an added edge in light of the 2010 revolt of African day laborers in the citrus groves of Calabria, who spoke back against inhumane living conditions, incessant racism, starvation wages and violent attacks. Indeed, the agricultural crisis affecting orange groves in southern Italy, once a thriving source of income, is largely the result of unregulated competition and misguided European Union agricultural policy. The irony is that without "illegal" African workers, agriculture in Calabria and Sicily would have collapsed long ago. Okudzeto's invocation of a global marketplace in the *Portes-Oranges* series touches directly on pressing concerns facing exploited Africans in Italy and their efforts to improve their living and working conditions in the face of growing hostility.

Persistent Stereotypes

The exhibition also unpacks several persistent stereotypes in Italian society and the sites associated with them. As Taiye Selasi demonstrates in her text in this volume, Italian men, in particular, have profoundly conflicted views of African women, denying them a public role as intellectuals. For *Nero su Bianco*, In-vernomuto creates a journey through the representation of the black female body in a specifically Italian context. Certain stereotypes shaping the Italian gaze were codified in nude photographs of Abyssinian women commissioned by Istituto Luce as part of the Fascist propaganda machine and in the Italian "Blaxpoitation" cinema of the 1970s, as well as Italian advertising in the 1980s. The demeaning imagery disseminated in earlier eras through public channels continues to reverberate in contemporary Italian society, resurfacing, for instance, in the censorious reactions of many public officials to the naming of Cécile Kashetu Kyenge, a Congolese Italian ophthalmologist and politician, as the Minister of Integration in the cabinet of Prime Minister Enrico Letta in 2013-14. This made her the first black cabinet minister in Italian history. Predictably, she became a lightning rod for harsh criticism and racist remarks, not so much for her advocacy of *jus soli*, which would grant citizenship to immigrants born on Italian soil, but because her public role as a policy maker confounded schemas that reduce women of color to sexual objects.

Adam Broomberg and Oliver Chanarin, whose work probes social injustice and political inequality, are represented here by a selection of images from their *Scarti* series. Created thanks to a sequence of accidents occurring when twice-printed scraps, the by-product of the photographic printing process, were saved rather than destroyed, the *Scarti* (short for *Scarti di avviamento*) feature uncanny combinations of images superimposed upon each other. In one, two men, one black and one white, wearing the same striped pajamas and standing in front of a green wall, seem to inhabit the same body. They are captured individually in the process of snapping a camera shutter with a remote shutter release, but the conflation of the two self-portraits has produced a moving tribute to their conjoined subjectivity. The elderly white man, who is largely subsumed into the form of the second figure, holds his extended arm holding the clicker high up away from his body, whereas the black man, staring straight at the camera, holds one hand pressed against his chest in a more reflective pose. It is as if, in the process of taking the picture, he recognizes himself and assumes an active role in determining his own identity. The play of arms evokes Eadweard Muybridge's photographs of people and animals in motion even as it emphasizes this self-recognition. The title, while referring to the printing process itself, also suggests discarded or marginalized people in Italian society, which is further underlined by *Ghetto*, the title of the book, which produced the recuperated double-printed sheets. But here Broomberg and Chanarin have created, even if by chance, a unique and moving testimony to a marginalized subjectivity escaping the confines imposed upon it.

Nari Ward's interactive sculptures entitled *Stallers*, on the other hand, seem to lull those lured into sitting in them into a "comfortable regression." Large baby stroller-like rebar constructions are fitted with hammocks, associated with idle repose, in the place of a padded baby seat, a crucial step for a child as it matures and asserts independence from parental control. Thus, Ward, in encouraging a condition of stasis, rather than movement, growth or maturity, posits waiting as a state of perpetual norm.

Laziness and inaction, of course, were pernicious stereotypes often applied to Africans as well as many Mediterranean peoples, including southern Italians, by those in the industrial north. The irony is that many enterprising Africans in Italy are now criticized not for their lack of initiative, but for their excessive zeal in succeeding in jobs that Italians have largely ceded to them. *Bamboccioni* — clumsy overgrown male babies still living with their parents well into adulthood — are a frequently lampooned phenomenon in Italian society. Statistics gathered in 2010 suggested that fifty percent of Italians aged 18 to 34 still lived with their parents. Ward turns the tables, creating a physical experience in which those reclining in his *Stallers* assume a stereotypical condition that is now more closely associated with white middle class Italians than it is with more recent immigrants. At the same time, Fred Kuwornu has called attention to the fact that many second-generation offspring of integrated immigrants find themselves in a kind of stalled limbo, lacking the rights of many of their Italian contemporaries.

During his year at the American Academy in 2001, Lyle Ashton Harris studied the Italian football stadium, which every Sunday becomes an inflammatory cauldron of performative masculinity, theatrical pageantry replete with Fascist salutes, slogans and chanting, and brutal racist taunting of non-white players. One of those athletes, Lilian Thuram, appears in one of Harris' photographs. A French player born in Guadeloupe, Thuram enjoyed a successful career with Italian clubs from 1996 to 2006. More recently, it has been talented players like Mario Balotelli — born in Palermo to Ghanaian immigrants, raised by Italian foster parents in Brescia and, since 2008, an Italian citizen — that have incensed mostly white football fans in Italy. Balotelli's agile, flamboyant style has earned him spots on the Italian national team, but his talent is frequently overshadowed by the reaction to the color of his skin. As the most prominent and most gifted player of African descent in Italy, but one with a volatile personality, who often speaks back to those criticizing him, Balotelli is an inevitable lightning rod for debates about integration and its effects on the national sport. It is not only fans who are guilty of deeply entrenched racism; a recently elected President of the Italian football association allegedly made a racist comment about a fictional African player, who went from "eating bananas" to playing for a team in Italy's premier league. The instances in which bananas are thrown onto the pitch, accompanied by choruses of insults, are too frequent to enumerate.

Jebila Okongwu takes the banana and its freighted symbolism as the key element in a work that tackles head on a series of stereotypes that are all too prevalent in Italian society. His work in various media, including sculpture, performance and painting, draws upon motifs reminiscent of his African heritage, namely the geometrical carving characteristic of tribal art from his father's native eastern Nigeria. He translates them into forms and objects made predominantly with colorful boxes for transporting bananas emblazoned with the logos of European fruit importers. He thus playfully sends up neo-colonial trade networks, the appropriations of Pop Art, as well as persistent racist stereotypes associated with the exotic other. For *Nero su Bianco*, Okongwu monumentalizes a pile of hand-crafted cardboard bananas arranged like the wares sold by the so-called *vu cumprà*, itinerant African street vendors. Installing them in the atrium of the McKim, Mead & White Building, the artist converts the standard accessory of a racist taunt into an accumulation of objects reminiscent of the *spolia* embedded in the walls of the Academy. While he decries tired assumptions that reduce African immigrants to purveyors of counterfeit designer handbags, and he is certainly sensitive to its power to offend, Okongwu nonetheless recuperates the banana and ennobles it as an African response to the antique fragments scattered around Rome.

The American Academy in Rome, an institution with a long tradition of fostering critical thought, offers a unique setting for this exhibition showcasing innovative work, much of it shown here for the first time, exploring race and identity in contemporary Italy. As the title suggests, the aim is to take a stand and open a wide-ranging cultural debate, rather than have the final word. The exhibition casts a probing eye on the complex factors — from the heritage of antiquity to the introduction of African American culture during World War II, from a colonial legacy to persistent stereotypes and the ongoing immigration crisis affecting the shifting demographics of not only Italy, but Europe as a whole — that have shaped perceptions of self and otherness. At the same time, it opens avenues for exploring new kinds of subjectivity and agency, plural points of view, that pave the way for institutions like the American Academy in Rome, in particular, and Italy more generally to be more inclusive and diverse laboratories for an ever-changing world.

1   Enwezor, O. (2006). "Repetition and differentiation — Lorna Simpson's iconography of the racial sublime", in Enwezor (Ed.), *Lorna Simpson* (p. 130). New York: Abrams.

2   See Christian Caliandro's essay in this volume.

3   "Afroitaliani: un sogno lungo un film?" *Cinemafrica. Africa e diaspore nel cinema* (3 October, 2008). See http//www.cinemafrica.org

4   Demby, W. (1996, 2 November), "An American Negro Survives," *East Hampton Star*, n.p.

5   Micconi, G. (2011). "Ghosts of History: An Interview with William Demby," *Amerikanstudien* vol. 56, no. 1, p. 126.

6   Demby, W. & Collins M. (1950, 18 November). "A.O. Nove anni dopo," *Epoca* vol. 1, no. 6, pp. 19-29.

7   Demby, W. (1996, 2 November). "An American Negro Survives," *East Hampton Star,* n.p.

8   Micconi, G. (2011). Op. cit., p. 134. On Demby's novels, see also Sherazi, M. M. "Posthumous Afterlives: Ecstatic Readings of Post-1945 American Literature." Ph.D. Diss. University of California, Riverside, 2015.

9   *Ibid.*, pp. 134-135.

10   Nowlin, M. E., (1991, April). "Lionel Trilling and the Institutionalization of Humanism," *Journal of American Studies* 25, no. 1, pp. 23-38.

11   See Giuliani, G., Lombardi-Diop, C. (2013). *Bianco e Nero. Storia dell'identità razziale degli italiani*. Milan: Le Monnier.

12   Micconi, G. (2011). Op. cit., p. 125.

13   *Ibid.*

Lyle Ashton Harris
Interview with
Frank M. Snowden, III

LAH   In co-curating the exhibition *Nero su Bianco* at the American Academy in Rome, I was inspired by your personal history as well as that of your immediate forebears, your grandfather Frank M. Snowden, Sr., and your father Frank M. Snowden, Jr. Let's start by discussing your time in Italy — what took you there initially?

FS   I first went to Italy in the summer of 1950, when I was four years old. My father was involved in a research project for three months. I have a few vivid memories: one is of the apartment where we stayed. I think that it was somewhere near Piazza Bologna. One clear recollection was of my birthday party, when I had *panettone* for the first time. I also remember having an Italian babysitter. She frightened me into good behavior by threatening that, if I misbehaved, she would call for the *polizia*. I didn't actually know what the *polizia* was, but that made the idea all the more frightening and mysterious.

LAH   What was your father's research focus at that time?

FS   I'm pretty certain that he was conducting research for *Blacks in Antiquity*. I don't know whether he had a fellowship or other institutional affiliation at the time. I had a much clearer understanding of what my parents were doing when we returned to Rome in 1954. As a result of my current research on the Cold War, I now have a much better idea of the work of the American embassy in that period. It's clear that Americans in the Fifties, especially African Americans, were becoming painfully conscious of the contradiction between the wartime language of the Four Freedoms and the reality of racial segregation in our country. The language was about democracy, but African Americans lived under a kind of totalitarianism in places like Mississippi and Alabama.

LAH   Can you explain the significance of the Four Freedoms?

FS   In 1941 President Franklin D. Roosevelt announced that the goal of World War II was to establish throughout the world freedom of speech, freedom of religion, freedom from fear, and freedom from want. I definitely think that African Americans had little idea of the meaning of freedom from fear or freedom from want, given the climate prevailing in the segregated South with its lynchings and the Ku Klux Klan. The abyss that prevailed between promise and reality was a major factor in the rise of the civil rights movement. African American soldiers returned from fighting abroad to destroy Nazism and racism only to rediscover that they were compelled to endure conditions that were unworthy of a civilized nation.

The U.S. State Department agonized over this contradiction, and what it might entail for America's position in the world — especially the battle for hearts and minds in Africa and Asia. This was even important background for the landmark case Brown v. Board of Education. In a number of cases leading up to Brown, the State Department actually submitted *amicus curiæ* briefs, arguing that America could never expect to compete in the Cold War unless something was done to change racial conditions in the United States. For the same reason the State Department decided that it was critical to find Asian Americans and African Americans to represent our country abroad, to demonstrate that times were changing. Fighting racism was a very important aspect of the political and diplomatic career of the American Ambassador to Italy, Clare Boothe Luce, the first American woman appointed to a major ambassadorial post abroad. The State Department sponsored trips abroad by African American intellectuals, artists, musicians, and athletes to underscore the point. Part of the magic of the Harlem Globetrotters was that they were a racially mixed basketball team. My father's first contact with the State Department was in the form of its recruitment of African American speakers to present their understandings of the problems of race relations in America, and of the slow and painful progress that was being made. As a leading educator, he also had the job of explaining the nature of an American liberal education. So before his tour of duty as cultural attaché in Rome, my father had served as a lecturer on exchange programs to India, to the Soviet Union, and to Africa. After those experiences he was offered the position of cultural attaché. There was a great sense of urgency to promote racial equality as a *sine qua non* of the Cold War. This had a direct and major impact on my father's life, and also on my own.

LAH   At the time there was a headline in *The New York Times* which read, "The U.S. Names Negro to Embassy in Rome" — it was the first such appointment to a major embassy post in Europe.

FS   His appointment was definitely a statement that times were changing. Clearly his academic standing as a classicist and an expert on Roman antiquity made him a logical and understandable choice. He was aware of the signifi-

cance of his appointment, and he meticulously saved the texts of his lectures and the reports that appeared about them in the Italian press, which covered them extensively. He was very proud of the fact that he lectured at every Italian university, and that he did so in Italian. The Italian reaction was overwhelmingly positive. As an African American with a prominent position in the American embassy, my father was a complete novelty. As a lecturer he was especially known for his energy and dynamism. He was even described in various articles as *il professore atletico* — a charac-

terization that even amused me at the time because he never had any interest in sports. Years later I remember attending some of his lectures at Howard University in Washington, D.C. My father was actually known as Zeus on campus because of his stentorian voice. When he lectured, people imagined that his words were like thunderbolts.

LAH   It's such a formative experience to live and attend school abroad when you're young. In the mid-Seventies when I was nine years old, my mother, brother and I moved to live in Dar es Salaam, Tanzania. How old were you when your family lived in Italy?

FS   At the time I was eight through ten-years-old, and I attended a private Catholic international school called Marymount. I had a sense of being almost in paradise; there was something utterly wonderful about growing up in Rome. My parents and my sister had a sense of that as well. Italian life is so richly textured. Because my own field study is modern Italian history, I know now that my parents' perceptions of Italy were a little different than mine. When my parents went to Italy from 1938 onward, they thought of the country as a place where the race question was non-existent. They knew, of course, about Mussolini's racial laws, but they regarded them as an abhorrent but temporary aberration that did not reflect the views of the Italian people. In Italy they felt free and welcomed.

The contrast with their experiences at home in the U.S. was stark. During the Thirties my father taught at Spellman College in Atlanta, Georgia, which my mother referred to as "the land behind the sun." What she meant was that, when my father went off to teach in the morning, she was never certain that he would come back alive. She was particularly concerned because my father could be argumentative, an "uppity African American" with a Boston accent who had little deference toward the peculiar customs of the South. After my parents' experiences in Atlanta, you can understand why their time in Rome proved to be so extraordinary and positive. As African Americans they felt totally accepted and free from American racial antagonisms. In the context of the Fifties that was powerful and profound, and even as a child I absorbed some of their feelings. Partly for reasons that I couldn't have articulated, I had an idyllic time in Rome, and my school there was welcoming and inclusive.

And my Italian experiences stood out in jarring contrast to the years that followed. Returning to the U.S. in 1956, I began a period of my life as a social experiment. The private schools in the Washington D.C. area were all segregated before 1956. In the wake of the U.S. Supreme Court ruling in Brown v. Board of Education, they collectively decided to integrate voluntarily. St. Albans, an Episcopalian school at the National Cathedral, began the process, and I entered sixth grade there as the first African American to attend a private school in the Washington D.C. area. But my entry to St. Albans was nothing like that of the African American students who integrated the public schools in the South. I can only imagine their courage and inner strength. There was never a time that I even thought about physical violence or feared for my safety. Nevertheless, my years at St. Albans — from 1956 to 1964 — were complicated and often psychologically painful.

LAH   Could you elaborate on that a little more? I think it's important to grasp your particular experience at such a highly charged time in American history.

FS   In 1956 the school wasn't fully prepared for the experiment on which it had embarked. Fortunately, there was never a problem with the teachers, all of whom treated me respectfully and fairly. But the administration hadn't really thought through the ramifications of what integration meant. One aspect of that lack of preparation was that they had never imagined the reactions of some of the students and their parents who were still committed to segregation. Another aspect that caught them off guard concerned issues that arose outside the school. In the Fifties and Sixties it was illegal to have racially mixed athletic competitions at schools in the neighboring states of Maryland and Virginia. On more than one occasion I was asked to stay behind instead of taking part in an event with the rest of my team. Similarly, when there were spelling bees, I never succeeded in making my class team, even though I was first in the class. When my father referred to such injustices, he used the word "irksome." Well, I also found discrimination irksome. It was also sudden and unexpected, infuriating and hurtful. The majority of the students in my class were accepting and friendly. Some of them became lifelong friends. But there was a minority of students who would make a point of sitting behind me in class to whisper "nigger" or to tell me to "go back to Africa."

LAH   That must have been quite traumatic. How did your parents and the school's administration respond to that situation?

FS   That's definitely a complicated question. An important point in understanding my parents is that they always believed in the vital importance of pressing forward with the great mission of integration. They believed profoundly that this was vitally important, and for that reason they were proud about what I was doing. Furthermore, they thought, like my grandfather, that the key to the future was the best education available. My father was quite passionately committed to that view. For those reasons, I think that my parents were often in denial about what happened to me at the school. There was also heavy pressure to succeed coming directly from the school's administration. When I was eleven years old I really believed and imagined that what happened to a whole people depended on me. In any case, to a limited, local extent, they meant it. In other words, St. Albans didn't actually admit another African American student until I was seventeen. So I was, in fact, an experiment, a test of one student marked out in the class of '52, in a school of several hundred students.

LAH   Do you think there was any relation between your father's denial of the racial abuses directed towards you in school and his own experiences of racial prejudice?

FS   An African American scholar who is halfway in age between my father and me made an observation that I've never forgotten. He said, "You know, Frank, there's a moving and poignant feature about the scholars of your father's generation at Howard [University]. On the one hand, they were extraordinarily strong and resilient. They had to be. But, on the other hand, there isn't one of them who wasn't spiritually mangled by the experiences they lived through." I thought that was a profound insight, and it certainly helps to explain the fact that my father was certainly in denial at times. His difficulties in dealing with my own struggles are a part of that.

There is an incident that took place in the Thirties when my father taught classics as a young assistant professor at Spellman [College] in Atlanta. During the school vacations he often drove back to Boston to see his family, and sometimes he gave a lift to two or three of his students. He recounted that on such trips there was a racial game one had to play, because it wasn't possible for an African American to stop just anywhere along the road for food or gas. On the contrary, he always had to remember to plan ahead so that he could stop in an African American neighborhood, because those were the only areas where it was possible to be served. On one occasion, however, he found himself running out of gas ahead of time. So he took the chance of pulling off the road at a random gas station somewhere in rural Georgia. There were three or four attendants standing around the pumps. When my father drove up, the one in charge said to another, "Go fetch my billy stick!" When he had it in hand, he came over to my father's window and said, "Now just what is it that you boys want here? You want gasoline, do you? Well, I'll just show you how I'll give you gas." And with that he poured gas all over the car, and then said, "If you nigger boys aren't out of here in ten seconds, I'm going to light a match!" As you might imagine, my father drove off at that point, gas or no gas. He and the three students sat in silence for some distance. This story illuminates how many of my father's generation were deeply scarred and spiritually mangled by such experiences, as well as the depth of his feeling in wanting the world to be a better place for the next generation, and for me. He couldn't bear the fact that things were just somewhat better; he wanted an entirely different world. It was awful for him to think that I may have had to live through such experiences. But that was a major difference between us; I never experienced the threat of physical violence or rarely feared for my safety.

LAH   Let's talk about your grandfather's and father's legacy, its fundamental challenge to tradition, and the way this culminates with you and your work.

FS   Their impact has been profound. I want to give voice to both my grandfather's and my father's views, even though they differ in some important ways from my own. I have a lot of respect for them, especially their attitudes on racial issues. It affects one of the two large intellectual projects that I hope to accomplish during my retirement. If my health and energy hold up, I would dearly love to write a three-fold collective autobiography of my grandfather, my father, and myself. It would be an attempt to make sense of our experiences over three generations. I don't believe that there is one compulsory way to be an African American. Each of us is different because there is no cookie-cutter way of forming an identity. I am, of course, different in many ways from those two Franks. On the other hand, there are many common threads and many similarities in terms of the issues that arose, and our reflections on them. So I thought that it would be interesting to write about the three of us. And this isn't intended as a slight to the women of our family — all of them were considerable figures in their own right. None of us would have been who we are without them. Nevertheless, at that specific time in history, there were certain distinct features particular to the African American males, and that's obviously the experience that I know best.

LAH   I'd like to learn more about your grandfather.

FS   My grandfather, Frank M. Snowden, Sr., whom everyone affectionately called "Colonel," maintained that the race question in America is never as simple as black against white, or the

39

Frank M. Snowden, Jr., Frank M. Snowden, III, and family with Pope Pius XII, c. 1955

other way around. The issue is far more complex and nuanced, because good and evil are randomly distributed among human souls. There was never a time when there weren't white people who supported the equality of African Americans, and there was never a time when there weren't African Americans who exhibited, like all people, certain social and personal pathologies.

I don't know whether "Colonel" read Du Bois. It's certainly possible, especially because he had a very clear vision of what Du Bois called the "talented tenth." In him it took the form of a passionate commitment that his two sons (he had no daughters) should have opportunities and successes that had been unavailable to him. Furthermore, he thought that it was the mission of his family to demonstrate in full public view that their genetic inheritance was second to none, that they could compete in any intellectual endeavor with anyone. As part of that "mission," my father did well at the Boston Latin School, where he won various awards, including the Franklin Prize. It was my grandfather's intention that my father should go to Harvard, that he should achieve excellence there as well, which he did, graduating in the class of '32, then going on to get his M.A. and Ph.D. degrees at Harvard as well. And the same applied to me as his grandson. He handed this message down through my father with the added proviso that I was responsible for doing better at Harvard than he had. The idea was ever onward, ever upward!

LAH   Your father's book, *Blacks in An-*

tiquity, was described by the *American Journal of Philology* as reflecting "exhaustive, impeccable scholarship." The *Boston Globe* noted its "scrupulous, balanced scholarship and quietly reasoned argument," and stated that his book "will be of lasting value not only to scholars but to anyone interested in questions of race and historical and social perceptions of race."

FS   *Blacks in Antiquity* received a very positive reception, both in terms of the reviews it attracted and in terms of sales to a broader public. My father be-

gan the work when he was still a doctoral student at Harvard. His dissertation, which he wrote in Latin, was a study of the foreign population at Pompeii. He was especially interested in people of African origin and the roles they occupied in ancient Roman society. This was the start of what became *Blacks in Antiquity.* At that time the role of people of color in the ancient world was essentially a non-subject. It was a question that very few people in classical studies were raising. By the Sixties, however, the impact of the civil rights movement and of the Cold War had transformed intellectual life, and in this new context the issues raised by my father's work were of burning interest and relevance.

LAH   Tell me about the impact of Italy on you in relation to your professional scholarship.

FS   By virtue of my father's work, I received powerful, positive messages about Italy, both consciously and unconsciously, and even some knowledge of the Italian language. Later on at Harvard, as a result of my major in Government, I developed an interest in the political sociologist Barrington Moore, Jr., and his interpretation of Fascism. What was missing in his work, however, was a discussion of Italy, and I thought that perhaps it would be interesting to explore Fascism in its Italian form. It helped that the country and the language were both familiar to me. It gave me the sense that this project was personally relevant to me, and that it was something that I had the preparation to master. So I returned to Italy as a result of an interest in studying Fascism, which became the subject of my doctoral dissertation. Having finished the doctorate, however, I discovered that I was smitten with Italy more broadly. I fell in love with the history of the country, its culture, its natural beauty, its food. My fascination with Italy lasted over the years because of a growing sense that Italian history is always contemporary in that it embodies some of the most pressing problems of today's world. Italy, in a sense, became for me a laboratory in which to test my understanding of the world around me.

An example of what I mean in this context is the way in which the problem of the North/South divide in Italy provides a window into issues of colonialism, under-development, and economic dualism. In much the same way, the Risorgimento and the problem of "making Italians" offer a perfect illustration of the difficulties and hazards of nation-building. Or I could argue that Fascism forces one to confront the larger general issues of racism, anti-Semitism, and political repression. Of course, not everyone would agree with me in my view of the deep connection between Fascism and racism. Indeed, if I may say so, I think that Italians have not yet come to terms with their fascist past and its legacy for the present.

A final illustration of my point is immigration, which is one of the most vexing issues of the modern world. Here Italy provides a perfect compendium of the issues at stake as a classic country of emigrants in the nineteenth and early twentieth centuries, and then, more recently, as a major country of immigrants. America and Italy both have long histories of dealing with the issue, and neither has yet resolved it in an inspiring and sustainable manner. Similarly, Americans are well prepared to understand Italy's sectional issue, the *Mezzogiorno*. Italy has not yet solved its southern question. The South is still economically, educationally, and socially disadvantaged, and there are still racial attitudes that inflame the relationships between northerners and southerners. That is an ongoing feature of the structure of modern Italian society and politics.

How is it possible that a country with such long and massive experience with the phenomena of immigration has not yet provided leadership in terms of devising wise and humane methods of dealing with it? How have Italians been so quick to forget their own past?

LAH What are some of the manifestations of this in contemporary Italy, for example the social anxieties around immigration that play out every day on the soccer field, as projected on the players?

FS People of color who play professional soccer in Italy are routinely jeered and booed, and the supporters' clubs backing many of the teams have been infiltrated by skinheads and neo-fascists. And violence, both verbal and physical, simmers just below the surface, sometimes erupting in ugly confrontations. This aspect of Italian life can be seen, for example, when the Neapolitan team plays Turin or Milan. Even without adding the presence of African players, the rivalry produces an explosive racial tension. When I first attended such a match, I was struck by the discovery that my study of medical history was surprisingly relevant. One of the insulting chants that the Turin fans used to demean the Neapolitans was to sing that they were uncivilized bearers of cholera. Asiatic cholera — that disease associated with filth, poverty, and the "Other" — was embedded in the northerners' serenade to the South! And although I personally have only rarely encountered virulent racial prejudice directed at me in Italy, I have seen and heard enough to realize that there is a current of racism that is ongoing today. I am also aware that it isn't something new. It didn't originate with the arrival of African immigrants, or with the Abyssinian War, or with Mussolini's

coming to power, even though those events were vitally important and added their own particular toxins to the mix.

LAH If we can digress for a moment, I would like you to share the story of your father's experience at the American Academy in Rome, which took place prior to his appointment by President Eisenhower as a cultural attaché to Italy. I think this recollection is significant in terms of taking an inventory of the Academy's institutional history.

FS Absolutely. But let's put this in the

context of a striking documentary film made in the Thirties when Mussolini visited the American Academy in Rome, which is in the archives of the Academy. Anyone watching the documentary can't fail to notice some salient features of the Academy in that period that seem foreign today, such as the fact that it was an exclusively male institution. A second feature is equally haunting, and in fact difficult to imagine. When Mussolini arrived at the Academy gate, and then again when he left, the

American fellows — or at least a depressingly large proportion of them — raised their arms in the fascist salute. How could they have done that? What did it mean?

Clearly the Academy today is a vastly different place. It is no longer a bastion of all-white male privilege. Obviously you and I would not be a part of an institution that was even remotely like that. To drive home further how profoundly the Academy has changed, I'll recount an incident that affected my father under the old regime that would never, ever happen today. During the Forties, my father had arranged to stay at the Academy, as what we would now term a "visiting scholar." In other words, he and my mother were paying guests while he conducted his research for *Blacks in Antiquity* in the Academy library, which is such a wonderful resource for classicists. At one point during his stay, the Academy director informed my father that there were Fellows from the South who refused to tolerate the idea of sharing living quarters with an African American. They told the director that they would leave the Academy if my father stayed. So the Academy director invited my father to leave and to stay in a hotel. This was a story that my father told me on several occasions, illustrating the negative side of a great institution at which he enjoyed working nevertheless. I should add that he was not especially critical of the Academy or believed that it deserved to be singled out; he simply thought it was reflective of American attitudes at that time.

LAH   Your personal history and its legacy have served as an implicit thread for me, both as a co-curator of the exhibition *Nero su Bianco* and as a fellow Trustee of the American Academy in Rome. Your scholarly contributions continue to be highly anticipated, and I am very appreciative of you sharing your candid reflections with me so graciously.

Echoes of Antiquity and Italian History

Carrie Mae Weems
The Edge of Time - Ancient Rome, 2006
Digital C-print
180×155 cm
Courtesy of the Artist and
Jack Shainman Gallery, New York

Justin Randolph Thompson
Loquens de Fluminibus, 2015
In costume, study for Super 8 film
Courtesy of the Artist

Barbara Chase-Riboud
Cleopatra's Bed, 1997
Multicolored bronze placques over steel
armature and silk mattress
60×120×60 cm
Courtesy of the Artist
and Michael Rosenfeld Gallery, New York

Elisabetta Benassi
Capo Portiere Bonjour, 2010
Hd video color sound transferred
on blu-ray disc on plasma wall
Duration 6' color
Dimensions variable
Courtesy of the Artist
and Magazzino, Rome

Onyedika Chuke
Studies for *The Untitled: 1919*, 2015
Graphite on paper
Courtesy of the Artist

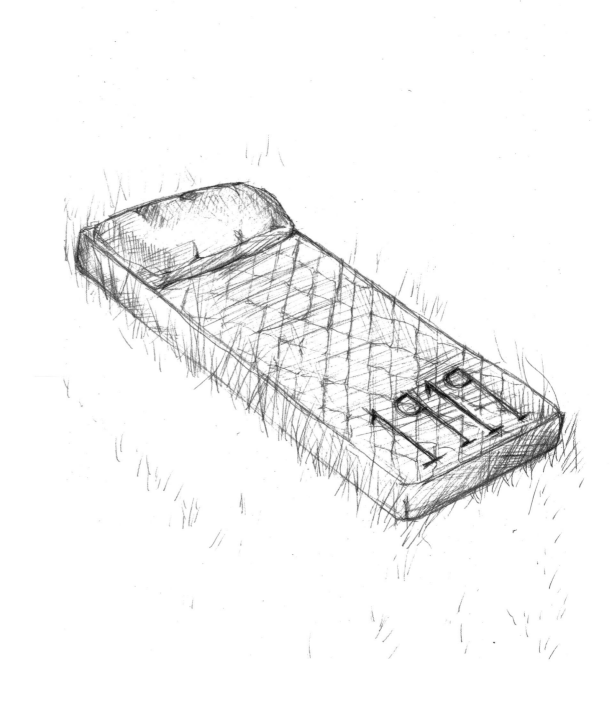

WORLD:
OF EMOTION

Benito Mussolini *Sigmund Freud*

AK 47

The Fascist Manifesto

The Uncanny

Mikhail Kalashnikov

–404 B.C.), when Athens and the
power in conflict, the Western
to Asia Minor under Alexander
:ored by the philosopher Aristotle
twenty-year-old Macedonian
›m Greece to India. A highly
·ating in every large city rapidly
throughout Persia and helped to
itities in history. Its life was
death, his generals divided this
spheres of influence.
style, Hellenistic sculptures like
phrodite and the *Borghese*
:ity and freedom resulting from
pace. A more revolutionary
f new themes, subjects and
e and public commissions
de-ranging, unexplored realm of
igs. These changes in form and
on from a civic-based art under
rsonal and individual approach

profound representations in art of
ted through the contorted faces
ie physical as well as psychic
unforgettable.

10. LAOCOÖN
C. 50–100 A.D.
(based on a Hellenistic sculpture)
Original marble;
Vatican, Rome

According to the Roman writer Pliny the Elder,
the *Laocoön* was "to be preferred to all that the
arts of painting and sculpture have produced."
For centuries, the opinion of Pliny remained
unchallenged. The powerful image of a priest
(punished for opposing the entry of the wooden
horse into Troy) and two sons struggling to free
themselves from serpents has left an indelible
mark on later generations of artists. The
sculpture, made from six blocks of stone, is one
of the most emotionally charged works in the
history of art.

Michelangelo saw the *Laocoön* at the site of
its excavation in Rome in 1505. He may have
been responsible for reconstructing the priest's
right arm. The *Laocoön* had a powerful influence
on Michelangelo, validating many important

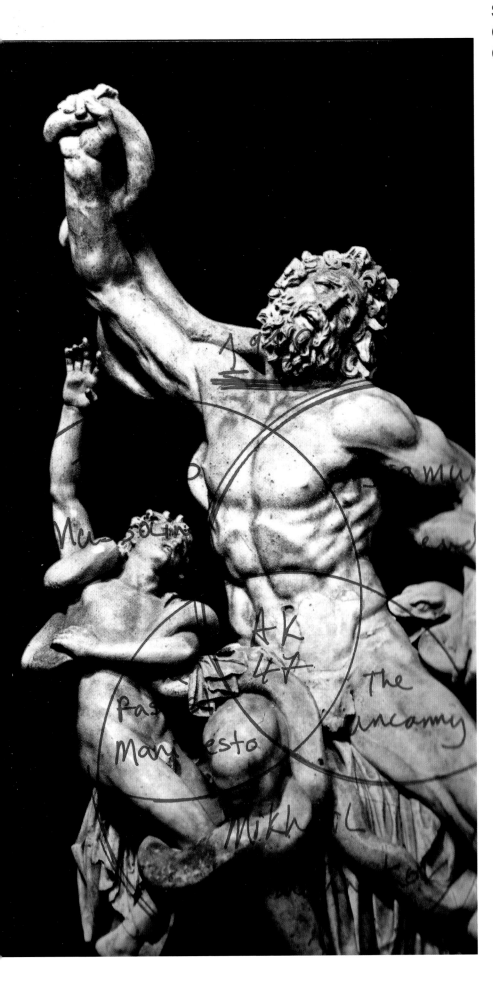

Onyedika Chuke
Studies for *The Untitled: 1919*, 2015
Graphite and ink on textbook page
Courtesy of the Artist

Meleko Mokgosi
Terra Pericolosa II (detail), 2015
Charcoal on paper
Dimensions variable
Courtesy of the Artist

Fred Wilson
Emilia's Mirror — Act 5, Scene 2, 2013
Murano glass and wood
203.2×124.1×27 cm
Courtesy of Pace Gallery

Vincenzo Latronico
First Person Colonial
with photographs by **Armin Linke**

Lake Assal, extraction of salt, Djibouti, 2012
C-print mounted on aluminum. Courtesy of Galleria Vistamare, Pescara

A few years ago I flew to Djibouti and slowly made my way along the abandoned railroad that leads to Addis Ababa through over a thousand miles of desert. My plan was to research a part of my family history — my mother was born in Ethiopia, and her Russian family had ties to that railway — and write a travel book in the process. I went with artist and photographer Armin Linke, and with a driver.

Back in Berlin I set down to writing, and my opening scene dawned on me with a self-evidence granted to few writers ... I would start with the time we almost got lost on our way to Lake Abbé, a salt lake in the middle of the desert, short on gas and sunset only a half an hour away.

I figured that scene would make an extremely fine beginning. It had actually happened, and included enough dramatic emphasis to catch the reader's attention. It was faithful to the experience of most Western travelers eschewing guided tours in unfamiliar far-away places. It respected that crucial aspect of travelogues — that of being healthy carriers of panoramas. The desert was indeed beautiful at that time of the afternoon, the horizon jagged with calcareous chimneys, dust settling behind us in the purple-blue sky.

Well, yes, it was. Yet it soon occurred to me that this wasn't the reason that

particular scene seemed so fitting as an introduction. Its main virtue was that of being a "hook" — it left the reader uncertain as to whether we would find shelter for the night and gas to continue our journey. I would thereby gain room for a flashback detailing the beginning of my trip without needing too many justifications — readers would simply be eager to get on with it in order to know the outcome (we did find the lake).

This is a ploy novelists often use in order to avoid that most painful of questions: "What is the point of all of this?", this *all* being a made-up plot about made-up characters. It is a writer's stratagem to exorcise fear. But what was I afraid of, just then? Shouldn't nonfiction have an inherent point in the fact that, well, it's real?

Not really. I was afraid of exoticism, or of its opposite. I was afraid I lacked enough experience of things Ethiopian, and of things human in general, to have anything meaningful to say about my experience there. I was afraid travelogues as a genre were inextricably tied to their origins, a time when a writer's account was the only way to learn something about a place and hence one had to make do with its inherent biases and limitations. I was afraid of unconsciously adopting the colonizer's gaze, of forcing everything I saw into a patched-up grid of excerpts from my anthropology syllabus, of ending up paralyzed in a post-colonial minefield in which my every move would betray the blind spots of my Western perspective.

This was a very sensible fear to have. My perspective there *could not* be but extremely limited, and only by denying this was the nineteenth century travelogue possible, in all of its authoritative naiveté. What I was ultimately afraid of, then, was to end up using Ethiopia to write about myself.

Actually, though, that was precisely what I was doing. I went to Ethiopia because my mother was born there; and my grandfather worked there as a lawyer under the Italian colonial administration; and my great-grandfather was sent there by Mussolini as the Emperor's attorney general for Italian Eastern Africa. He made a name for himself by arguing that, if an Ethiopian witness refused to cooperate with Fascist authorities in the investigation of a crime, the punishment would strike the whole village where the crime had taken place. This was what drew me to Ethiopia.

This line of thought kept me paralyzed for a while. In the hope of finding a way out, I thought I'd tackle the project differently — I'd begin by reviewing the photographs that would go in the book. I met Armin Linke in his Berlin studio to check out the pictures he'd shot. I sat down in front of dozens of pages of contact proofs, with a beer and a sheet of green stickers. "Put one on the pictures you like," Armin said.

After a few minutes of speechless leafing through, I realized I would mark none of them — I was dealing, once again, with the same problems that were keeping me from writing. The pictures I liked were invariably banal, postcard-like — even I recognized them as clichés.

"Sorry," I said with a short laugh, as if apologizing for my indecision. "I'm not very refined. The ones I like are just dramatic landscapes, colorful street markets, you know, like, picturesque stuff."

Armin seemed to ponder for a few seconds.

"You know, maybe we shouldn't be interested in avoiding the picturesque."

In my view, focusing on the Djibouti-Addis Ababa railway was a less arrogant approach to the travelogue, and a way to avoid wandering in idleness, collecting panoramas. It was an approach to the Western presence in Ethiopia outside of the strictly colonial framework: the corporation was actually a partnership between the Ethiopian Empire and some Western investors, including my Russian ancestors.

My maternal grandmother was raised in Addis Ababa after fleeing the Russian revolution in 1917. Her father had been in business with the Emperor, and asked for hospitality to spare his family the hardships other Russian émigrés were facing in Paris and London. They lived for two decades as the Emperor's guests,

Digital stock market ticker for coffee, Harar, Ethiopia, 2012
C-print mounted on aluminum. Courtesy of Galleria Vistamare, Pescara

the sole white members of the Ethiopian court. When the Italian invaders arrived they switched sides immediately, and my grandmother was quickly married off to the son of one of the highest Fascist officials. After the Italians were vanquished, she was granted a sort of pardon, and while her husband languished in a prison camp in Kenya, she taught French at a local school for blind girls. This was the story I wanted to track down.

I flew to Djibouti with a bag full of photographs, old documents and letterheads — threads that, if uninterrupted, would have allowed me to recover something that I believed to be mine. But the threads were interrupted, or that thing did not belong to me. The only traces I found of the five decades my family spent there were a couple of sentences whispered by an old Armenian shop owner — wrapped tightly in the myriad layers of his white-linen *shamma* — who remembered dancing once with my grandmother. If he misremembered, which he very well might have, the whole story of my family in Ethiopia could even have been invented.

However, it was not. What had happened, instead, is that it was not *preserved*: its traces were not retained as it continued elsewhere.

When, in the attempt to find the location of my family home, I visited the national telephone company asking if somewhere they had a phone book from the Sixties, all of the employees started laughing. Their laugh didn't mean, as it would have in Italy, that it was surely somewhere, since someone would have kept it, but who knows where. It meant they were sure none would be around, since they found it *useless*. "For what

purpose?" asked a clerk that I talked with. "There's a new one; it's on DVD."

This was particularly striking in the case of the railway. Given the antiquity of the project and its relevance to the modernization of Ethiopia, we expected to find a documentation department, even just a photographic collection: but we did not. Our questions on this matter were met with a specific mix of incomprehension and amusement. We did find old documents — even some original blueprints dating back to the beginning of the twentieth century — but they were kept only because they had been updated: they were old but still in use. The idea of storing obsolete charts or manuals already supplanted appeared as a joke. To the eyes of our interlocutors, the archive that we were looking for was a sort of cemetery, a place designated uniquely to keep papers once there was no more reason to keep them.

I got to Ethiopia expecting an archival mindset: the idea that every scrap of paper can be construed as a historical document that, as such, needs preserving (bills, school report cards, medical files, old contracts). This mindset posits history as a transitive property: macro-history, the so-called History with a capital H, is composed of "small" events that are nonetheless just as historical and hence must be kept for some future researcher.

This, of course, is a retrospective rationalization. Old contracts, birth certificates and medical files weren't kept in the European past as a treasure trove for later historians, but as a means of organization and control. Empires have always been very good at paperwork. In this context, deleting traces can be seen as an adaptive, anti-authoritarian strategy for a country that has seen five contrasting regimes in a single lifetime.

Moreover, this lack of an archival necessity might have something to do with the relationship Ethiopia has with the idea of progress. Haile Selassie had originally theorized an "Ethiopian way" to modernity, one proceeding at a slow but constant pace; but this was later billed as regressive, and too slow, by the communist Derg. Today, the struggle to keep up with globalization is often seen as an impossible task. Under this light, a past that has no use value triggers feelings of shame, a sensation of being backward, rather than a desire to preserve for future reference.

The regime changes have instilled the habit of erasing and rewriting. Each new layer encourages forgetting the previous one, because it is based on the principle of its uselessness, on the convenience and need of "leaving behind." Of course, nothing is really left behind.

After setting up their headquarters in the Emperor's palace, in Addis Ababa, Italian occupants saw it fit to build a monument marking the beginning of their Empire: a concrete staircase, spiraling up around an empty flagpole. Each step represented an additional year in the Age of Fascism, which had started in 1922.

I have a hard time understanding what positive message could have been gleaned from the image of a staircase that ends nowhere and leads those who climb it to step abruptly into the void. In its makers' intentions, the monument's inherent incompleteness had something dynamic, it expressed a lingering upward tension: we rise, and rise, and shall never be stopped!

But of course they were stopped, after a mere nineteen steps. However, Haile Selassie, upon reconquering his former palace, elected not to destroy his enemies' monument; instead, he placed on the top step a small statue of a lion — his throne's symbol.

In a stunning *détournement*, the void behind it now signals an interruption, a broken promise of continuity. Without changing physically, that stair-

Colonial Fascist sculpture, with the Ethopian Lion
of Judah, Ethnographic Museum, Addis Ababa, Ethiopia, 2012
C-print mounted on aluminum. Courtesy of Galleria Vistamare, Pescara

case became a ruin of itself, a memento of the end of what it was meant to celebrate. That is, well, us.

I didn't know what to expect as an Italian traveling in a former colony; even now I have a hard time interpreting the few interactions in which it became apparent. They took place mostly in Harar — maybe because the distance from the capital has softened, over the decades, the memory of the atrocities enacted by the central power.

In Harar we were often addressed in Italian by older men on the street. They seemed proud of their knowledge of our language and eager to talk about their memories. They kept insisting that the Italian colonization was "an engineers' colonization," that only the French and the British came with soldiers instead. We didn't know whether this was said to humor us, or whether it was an effect of the continuous revisions of history over several regime changes, or just old age seeing youth as better anyway.

A man we met in the garden of the Harar beer brewery explained to us at length that Ethiopia was a privileged colony, since the only other place colonized by Italians had been America five hundred years earlier. He then started chanting *Faccetta Nera*, a fascist anthem. We recognized it even though

we'd never heard it, since it is now forbidden by law on Italian soil. He knew the words by heart.

And those words kept haunting us — our own words, but slightly warped and twisted: in conversations we overheard, in fast-paced dialogue on television or the radio. This must be extremely banal for native English speakers, intrinsic to

any experience abroad: you're in a faraway place where you don't know the history or language, foreign-looking individuals are discussing some unfathomable local business when all of a sudden they switch to speaking *your mother tongue*. It's just a few words, maybe a phrase, and the pronunciation is weird and unplaceable (as with words like film, computer, dollar): and yet you have no doubt what it is.

On the other hand, north of the Alps and south of the Mediterranean, Italian usually shrinks down to a few dozen terms (among them *pizza*, *biennale*, *omertà*). Realizing someone from another part of the world is speaking what until then was simply *your* language is a powerfully disorienting experience. All the more so because it takes a while for the reason to sink in; it takes a while for you to realize why, exactly, it is your language they speak there.

"Excuse me, could I have a toothpick?"

"Sorry?"

"A toothpick? A small stick made of wood, for my teeth?"

"Sorry? I don't understand."

I point at a toothpick.

"Ah! Stekkino!"

"Yes, stekkino, thank you very much."

Italians never speak of colonialism; they don't study it at school, they don't remember it on special dates and occasions, they do not reconstruct it through monuments and museums. Italians do not fancy themselves "real" colonizers; the fallout of the Fascist regime during the second half of the last century effectively prevented any collective elaboration of guilt.

We shrug and sort of smile as if to say we're good for nothing, we've lost every war, how bad could it have been? So we hide behind the comfortable illusion that since our colonial expansion was smaller and less successful than that of Britain or France, the atrocities committed in its name must have been proportionally scaled down; or that our ineptitude prevented us from making too much damage anyway.

The point is that the analytical process of decolonization hasn't even started. This is painfully clear on a national, collective scale: a small town in central Italy recently devoted a monument to Rodolfo Graziani, the Fascist viceroy who committed genocide in Ethiopia. But even without going to such extremes, even individually, even in myself, all my carefulness and readings notwithstanding, this lack has sometimes been dramatically evident. A couple of months after coming back, I was talking about my trip with a Ghanaian translator I had met at a conference. I told her, among other things, that my grandfather had been in a prison camp after the British had freed Ethiopia from Italians. It's what my mother and my history classes had told me.

"It wasn't the British who freed Ethiopia," she said. "It was the Ethiopians."

And so on, and so on.

I was reviewing the proofs for my travelogue when my mother sent me a manuscript by my maternal grandmother Marina Ivanovna Kvostoff. She had transcribed it years ago on an early computer and had kept a printout in her papers. She thought she'd lost it; I didn't even know it existed. It is another way of writing about Ethiopia.

The title is *Ethiopia Hoy!*, the opening line of the Ethiopian national anthem under Haile Selassie. The manuscript is the diary of Shoushanik, a white Armenian teenager raised in Ethiopia, kept during the Italian occupation. Shoushanik's family had ties to Ethiopian high society, but their status as Westerners made the household a sort of neutral ground during the regime change.

Shoushanik has strong ties to the Amhara aristocrats — both her best friend and her lover, Lij Amdé, are among

Meskel Square, Addis Ababa, Ethiopia, 2012
C-print mounted on aluminum. Courtesy of Galleria Vistamare, Pescara

its members — and she soon ends up serving as a spy for the Ethiopian insurgents. Shoushanik's family, however, hosts some Italian officers and one of them, captain C., starts courting her and is not wholly unwelcome.

Shoushanik is torn between two contrasting feelings: her fidelity to the culture she loves and grew up in, but which nonetheless never wholly accepted her; and her attraction to a world that claims her as a part of itself, but in so doing slaughters the people to whom she's closest.

Graziani's massacre forces a resolution. Shoushanik learns Amdé had attempted to murder the viceroy and hides him in her rooms; the Italian captain discovers him but ultimately agrees to let him go, even though they are rivals both at war and in love. In so doing he wins Shoushanik's heart, but it is unclear whether her feelings are genuine, or a reward, or a ransom. In any event, the two men disappear in the turmoil of war, and Shoushanik ends up homeless and alone, roaming through Europe to forget a country that had never been hers, two men, and an abortion.

The novel ends in Rome, where my grandmother moved after the second Communist uprising in her life kicked her out of Ethiopia. There, she worked for three decades for the Tolstoy founda-tion, assisting refugees from the Soviet Bloc; she lost her husband prematurely, weakened by the hardships he had endured in the prison camp; and she died, in 2005, and was buried in the Non-Catholic cemetery, halfway between Keats, whom she probably loved, and Gramsci, whom she most certainly did not.

I cannot really speak to the novel's value — it was autobiographical and naïve and often extremely touching. The narrator is impossibly neutral vis-à-vis the story she relates, and this neutrality is the result of opposing forces. Shoushanik is both extremely aware of what she's talking about and completely unaware (hypocritically so?) of her own prejudice. My grandmother Marina fled to Ethiopia when she was three and stayed there until she was fifty; she wore a *shamma* more often than a scarf; the land and the culture she felt as her own. Under many aspects, she identified as an Ethiopian woman, but of course she wasn't.

And yet she hadn't gone there as other Westerners had, looking for money or power: she had been a welcome, if ultimately ungrateful, guest. Maybe this means her position was a little less compromised — although I'm not sure. Her sense of belonging, her knowledge and love are evident in the way her novel devotes long descriptions to the Ethiopian landscape, language and peoples. However, it is equally clear that my grandmother also felt a different kind of affiliation, a sort of closeness to the invader.

This is apparent in the novel's plot: falling in love with the Italian captain isn't seen as a betrayal, so much as an unavoidable fate — as if some sort of blood affinity finally trumped the narrator's love for Amdé and for Ethiopia.

It would be easy to blame this outcome as hypocritical and self-serving, and the book, under this perspective, is a document of such hypocrisy. Prejudiced speech often starts out with a declaration of love. But this is not only a document: it is also a novel about a twenty-year old woman in love, written by a sixty-year old woman who reminisces about the country where she spent most of her life without ever fitting in, a country she would never visit again, just like she never visited Russia while nonetheless abstractly calling it home.

Under another perspective, then — narrower, perhaps, but in a way deeper — one could simply consider with curiosity and tenderness this instance of emotional dissonance; any moral judgment being implicit in the decision to avoid repeating it. Ethiopia has changed two more anthems since then.

This text was excerpted and translated from Latronico, V., Linke, A. (2013). *Narciso nelle colonie. Un altro viaggio in Etiopia.* Macerata: Quodlibet Humboldt.

The Colonial Legacy

Theo Eshetu
The Return of the Axum Obelisk, 2009
Video installation
Dimensions variable
Courtesy of the Artist

Alessandro Ceresoli
Linea Tagliero - Prototipo 04, 2009
Glass, mirror in two parts
86×116.2×31.6 cm
105.7×84.5 cm
Courtesy of the Artist

Alessandro Ceresoli
Bloody Thirty Years, 2009
Black marker on paper, gold leaf
134.5×115.5 cm
Courtesy of the Artist

ASSASINATION OF ASMARA'S ARCHITECTURE AND URBAN PLANNING WAS CONFRONTED WITH THE FASCIST ERA, RACE DIVISIONS, AND THE AVANGARDE CLAIMS OF MODERNISM. ERITREA WAS ANNEXED BY ETHIOPIA IN 1961, WHICH AGAIN CAUSED A BLOODY 30 YEARS LIBERATION WAR RESULTING IN THE INDEPENDENCE OF ERITREA IN 1991. ITALY'S EXPANSIONIST POLICIES TOWARD ETHIOPIA AND THE ENSUING WAR USING LETHAL GAS WEAPONS THUS, THE FASCINATION OF ASMARA BOOMED IN THE 1930s AS A COLONIAL METROPOLIS THE REASON FOR THIS BOOM WAS

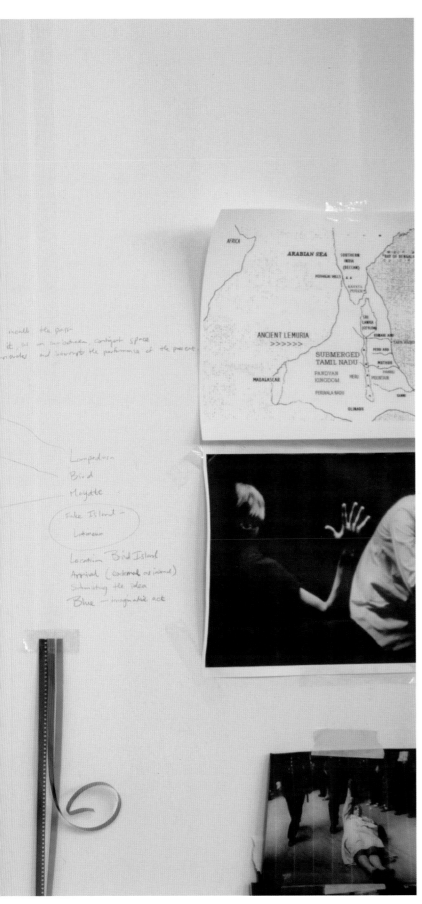

Bridget Baker
*E dovunque (in search
of an untailored account),* 2014 onwards
8mm film leader, a map of Lemuria and
printouts of research images made with
an iPhone stuck to a wall in the artist's
studio in London

*E dovunque (in search
of an untailored account),* 2014 onwards
Detail of printouts of research images
made with an iPhone stuck to a wall in the
artist's studio in London
Italian audience claps after watching
a screening of *Africa Addio* in 1966

*E dovunque (in search
of an untailored account),* 2014 onwards
Detail of printouts of research images
made with an iPhone stuck to a wall in the
artist's studio in London
Franco Prosperi answers questions about
the film *Africa Addio* during a trial debate
organized by *La Tribuna Illustrata* in
Rome in 1966

Senam Okudzeto
Mini Mundus, 2011
Iron, blue paint, oranges
65×45 cm
Courtesy of the Artist

Senam Okudzeto
I asked him, more, 2014
Acrylic, black ink, tracing paper,
collage, Arches watercolor paper
26×18 cm
Courtesy of the Artist

Lyle Ashton Harris
Appunti per l'Afro-Barocco, 2015

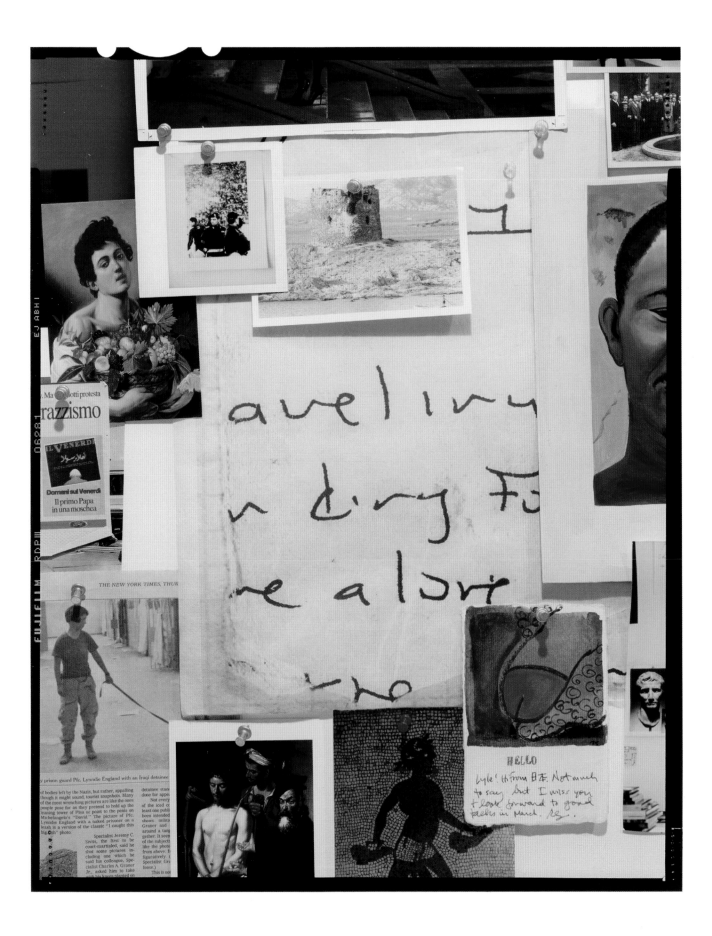

95

96

Christian Caliandro
*African Italian Identity in Italian
Cinema and Literature, 1946–1982*

Nobody knows
the troubles I've seen
nobody knows
my sorrow.
Joe In *Paisan*
(Roberto Rossellini, 1946)

They will destroy Rome
And upon its ruins
They will lay down the seed
of the Ancient History.
Pier Paolo Pasolini,
Prophecy (1965)

The elaboration of African Italian identity in the cultural imaginary of the Italian nation is above all a matter of a constructed gaze: how collective perception is shaped around this new object, through cultural and spectacular production, and, in particular, in the disciplines of cinema and literature. This elaboration is part of a wider process of intellectual discovery and narrative exploration linked to the development of the social, political, economic world in postwar Italy.

Italian Neorealism consists mainly, if not exclusively, of a reconstruction of a cultural gaze on reality. Italy was able to rebuild its own identity looking at the tragedy of this reality, not denying it or refusing it: that "degree zero" was not a mere hypothesis, but the actual condition of a national community.

Furthermore, it was necessary to train and educate the gaze, after a period of twenty years in which it had withered, in order to form a new point of view to comprehend a country that had remained hidden from itself for so long. And this adjustment deeply influenced the formulation of the collective self; it provided the basis of every subsequent transformation, perception and projection. So, the birth of Neorealism represents the radical transformation of an entire perspective, and of the paradigms through which Italians viewed and interpreted reality around them. Film director Ermanno Olmi described this process, which he experienced directly as a teenage viewer confronted by Rossellini's masterwork: "Back then I discovered that two types of cinema existed: a mushy, pleasant representation of reality, and a total correspondence between what was inside and outside of the movie theatre, which led the viewer to recognize himself *within* reality."[1]

Until that moment, Italian cinema had been dominated by the so-called *telefoni bianchi* (white telephone) films, imitations of American comedies of the Thirties, offering an artistic form of escapism, made of romantic sequences set in exotic and imaginary places. The function of cinema before the war was in fact the creation of a collective dream, of *another* dimension to live in, temporarily abandoning the real world outside the movie theaters. *Rome, Open City* provoked a shock to culture and representation because it activated the opposite process, that is a total identification between the reality projected on the screen and that *outside* the theater, a process also leading to *recognition* through which one succeeds in positioning oneself in the world, in the same reality depicted on the screen. Through this operation, one that is absolutely not mechanical, viewers become aware of who they are, moving towards a fuller understanding of their individual and collective existence.

Paisan (1946), the second chapter of Roberto Rossellini's "Anti-Fascist War Trilogy," widens the gaze to the whole Italian peninsula fighting for its liberation (a similar phenomenon, but on a continental scale, can be seen two years later in *Germany Year Zero*): the fragmented structure of the episodes, each dedicated to a city or to a geographical area of the country from north to south, paradoxically makes the narrative extremely cohesive. In particular, the second episode about Naples is a perfect mix of humanity, humor, tragedy and documentary approach. The encounter between the Military Policeman Joe and Pasquale the street urchin strikes the viewer for its simple but precise investigation of a cultural clash. In the physical and psychological urban context of the bombed buildings, Joe, drunk, tells his "long, fantastic lie" about his homecoming; then the kid steals his shoes. During their next encounter on the street a few days later, the kid takes Joe to see where he lives: a hovel, a sort of cave where many refugee families live together, a traumatic environment that suddenly cancels any distance and incomprehension. This space is portrayed as it appears in many literary texts of the period (from *Kaputt* and *The Skin* by Curzio Malaparte to *Parliamo dell'Elefante* by Leo Longanesi, from *Fuga in Italia* by Mario Soldati to *Naples '44*, a memoir by Norman Lewis).

Soon after, the reconstruction of Italian cinema as a production apparatus materialized in the "Hollywood sul Tevere," an entire world modeled within the bright and vibrant Rome of the postwar period, which contributed to the formation of a unique cultural fabric. In 1951 Mervyn LeRoy directed *Quo Vadis?* at Cinecittà, a project that marked the official beginning of a highly success-

ful new genre, the *peplum* film. These movies, also known in Italy as *sandaloni*, proliferated during the Fifties (*Ben Hur*, shot in 1959 by William Wyler, being the most notable), and reached their golden age during the Sixties. They were very rudimentary historical or mythological narratives, often focused on the character of the "strong man" (Maciste, Ursus) and were generally produced on a limited budget. The genre was responsible for the introduction of African American actors — who often played the roles of slaves, gladiators or leaders — into the production system of Italian cinema. Among this group, the most singular figure was Harold Bradley: an extraordinary and interdisciplinary character who could confidently shift from art, to acting, to musical performance. After having played in the NFL with the Cleveland Browns (with whom he won two Super Bowls), he moved to Italy in 1959, initiating his career in the film industry. Among his roles were those in *Io, Semiramide, servo di Semiramide* (1962), *Maciste il gladiatore più forte del mondo* (1962), *Il gladiatore di Roma* (1962), *Cleopatra* (1963), *Maciste l'eroe più grande del mondo* (1963), *L'eroe di Babilonia* (1963), *Jason and the Argonauts*, (*Gli Argonauti*, 1963), *Maciste nell'inferno di Gengis Khan* (1964) and *La caduta dell'impero romano* (1964). Later, he interpreted one of the *Seven Rebel Gladiators* (*Sette gladiatori*, 1965), directed by Michele Lupo. Meanwhile, Bradley cultivated his interest for African American music, and through it approached the Civil Rights movement. Besides painting, he also took up singing, and transformed his art studio into the *Folkstudio*, a venue for concerts and social meetings that proved fundamen-

Pier Paolo Pasolini, *Notes towards an African Orestes*, 1970, film still

tal in conveying jazz and folk music to an Italian audience. It went on to become one of the most important crossroads for musical, artistic and cultural life in Rome during the Sixties. Bob Dylan, Ravi Shankar and Pete Seeger, among others, performed there.

While until this moment the perception of African Italian identity was configured in Italian popular culture primarily at the level of everyday life, during the second half of the Sixties, Pier Paolo Pasolini's work effected an important intellectual turn destined to exert a profound and durable influence on Italian collective conscience. His *Prophecy* (1965), included in *Alì dagli Occhi Azzurri*, represents the lucid examination of a historical, social and economic process that involves different peoples confronting each other, as well as diverse and opposed civilizations: "Alì with his Blue Eyes / one of the many sons of the sons / will descend from Algiers, on / rowboats and ships.

Thousands of men / will be with him / with the little bodies and the eyes / on boats launched in the Kingdom of Hunger. They will bring children with them, / and bread and cheese, in the yellow paper of Easter Monday. / They will bring grandmothers and donkeys, on the triremes stolen from the colonial ports. / They will unload in Crotone or in Palmi, / in millions, wearing Asian wrecks, and American shirts."[2]

Africa and "negritude," for Pasolini, cross continental borders, and outline

an entire cultural alternative, a possible collective identity that involves the whole South of the world (the outskirts of Rome, Southern Italy, Spain, Greece, the Middle East) being transfigured by a return to archaism as a resistance to ongoing transformation: "always modest / always weak / always shy / always lowest / always guilty / always subject / always tiny, / they who never wanted to know, they who had eyes only to beg, / they who lived like killers underground, they who live like outlaws / at the bottom of the sea, they who lived like crazies in the sky / they who built laws outside of the law / they who adapted to a world underneath the world..."[3].

So, in the second half of the Sixties, Pasolini, as a writer and director, worked to clarify this intuition and to articulate this observation, collecting ideas and searching for material. An essential part of this reflection is manifest in the movies *Medea* (1969), *Notes Towards an African Orestes* (1970) and *The Walls of Sana'a* (1971). As Enzo Siciliano writes, "Medea incarnates prehistory, where life is only about sense, and where nature is a stack of black and inexplicable forces. Magic is Medea's culture. (...) In Medea, in her desperation, Pasolini represented his own cultural desperation — but sealing it in myth, soaking it in the outdated quality of decadent figuration."[4] Medea, with her "weight of gems and precious stones, of black and bristly clothes",[5] symbolizes all the aspiration to the primitive and the irrational that characterizes the visual arts and the cinema of the late Sixties. These sparks are developed in *Notes Towards an African Orestes*, a non-linear and informal narrative realized in the form of a diary retracing the trip in the obscure heart of Africa with Alberto Moravia with original shots and found footage. The *Notes* delineate a complex discourse, developed on the model of Æschylus' tragedy, about the conflictual relationship between irrational forces, the "Furies" — narratively and visually identified here in the gigantic trees that stir in the wind, "the monstrous anthropomorphic roots" (Enzo Siciliano)[6] — and the rationality of human justice, symbol of the ascendant Western civilization. "Realistic" and "true" are equivalent here to "mythical" and "sacred." The most interesting section — together with the jazz session of Gato Barbieri, who composed the movie's soundtrack, with Yvonne Murray and Archie Savage (recorded at Bradley's *Folkstudio*) — is the one dedicated to the discussion with the African university students at La Sapienza: while Pasolini interrogates them on the plausibility of the transposition of the Greek tragedy to the Africa of the Sixties, the African students, already integrated into Italian society, explain very politely but firmly that post-colonial reality was far more complex than one resulting from an interpretation in such imaginative terms.

Thus, it is striking to recognize the same ideas, figures, and scenes from Pasolini's movie reflected in the first of three books about Africa published by Alberto Moravia, *A quale tribù appartieni?* (1972), which recalls specific places and objects: "Later, we waited as Pier Paolo Pasolini (the movie he is shooting for Italian television was the excuse for my journey to Tanzania) carefully photographed the African landscape (circular villages of the Maasai people, huge monstrous baobab trees, fantastic piles of stones similar to colossal mangoes gathered by the hand of a giant)."[7] The central idea of the whole discourse, written in the form of a travel journal, concerns Africa as the place of "prehistory": "History, in Europe and in Asia, doesn't seem to weigh heavily; you would say that it is in the air. But when you find yourself in Africa, the relief that you feel demonstrates that West and East are intoxicated by history. Prehistory, despite its terrors, can seem like a refuge."[8] From this point he developed a conception of an African identity understood as complementary to the European and Western one, from an Italian point of view: "(...) the African man is not 'different' from the European man, he is not an 'other.' He is simply the other face of the European, his completion, his alternative."[9]

This alternative — as for Pasolini, but with a surplus of anthropological attention — is made up of archaism, and of magical culture. For example, describing "*ju-ju*" practices and African masks, Moravia outlines the "faintness of individual identity," one that always risks becoming blurry and disappearing: "Maybe it is not an immediately terrifying mask; but finally it is unbearable for me to look at it. Indeed, this mask doesn't want to frighten, it 'is' fear itself. The faintness of the human being that scares Africans so much is expressed by the body transformed into a sheaf. The face, closed in the stocking covered by shells like an underwater reef, alludes to the inability of man to emerge with his face from a proliferating and overwhelming nature."[10]

These types of reflections, in both cases, are part of a horizon of ethnographic intellectual research connected, for example, to Claude Lévi-Strauss' *The Savage Mind* (1962), translated into Italian in 1964, but also to Ernesto De Martino's *Sud e Magia* (1959), which introduced these issues into an Italian context in the same period. The latter is about the swerve of civilization, and the necessity of looking at a culture that functions with its own structured rules, with its own "socialized and traditionalized techniques:" "Now, the protective function of magical practices is inserted in these conditions of faintness of the presence. Magic (...) is a set of socialized and traditionalized techniques oriented towards protecting presence from the crisis of 'psychological misery' and to open again, thanks to this protection, realistic operative forces. In an existential regime where the power of negation involves the center of cultural positivity, that is to say presence as an operative energy, the use of man's technical power preserves value and function, not for producing economic material goods, or the material and mental tools for a better control of nature, but for the defense of that

fundamental good that is the condition of participation, as narrow as it may be, in cultural life."[11]

Moravia narrated his connection to Africa in two other volumes, *Lettere dal Sahara* (1981) and *Passeggiate africane* (1987): the most interesting and relevant aspect of this production, as in the case of Pasolini, is his capacity to widen the "Neorealist" literary gaze from the Italian context to that of another continent. The ability to extract an entire world of social and political

connections, of historical and economic transformations changing the face and the identity of Africa, from the smallest details and fragments of humanity, collected during these physical and mental journeys. Starting from Rossellini's model, Neorealism is configured as a way of comprehending the world, before narrating it — a cognitive tool as well as a narrative one.

Completely different is the impact exerted by black actors on the *poliziotteschi* films, which characterized Italian popular culture in the Seventies, but it is equally relevant to the construction of African Italian identity in the collective imaginary. The actor who epitomizes perhaps more than anyone else this type of spectacular figure is Woody Strode. He played Stony in the legendary first sequence of the arrival of the train in *Once Upon a Time in the West* (Sergio Leone, 1968), and interpreted Masinissa in *Scipione detto anche l'Africano* (1971), directed by Luigi Magni, the Berber prince who constantly reminds Scipio-Mastroianni of the glory and the greatness of the battle of Zama. After these roles, the American actor performed the role of one of the two killers in *Manhunt* (*La Mala Ordina*, 1972), the masterpiece by Fernando Di Leo and central part of his "Trilogia del milieu," which also included *Caliber 9* (*Milano Calibro 9*, 1972) and *The Boss* (*Il boss*, 1973). Strode also played in the apocalyptic spaghetti-western *Keoma* (1976), directed by Enzo G. Castellari, which marked the last gasp of this genre.[12] Castellari directed Fred Williamson, another African American actor often present on Italian screens, in *The Inglorious Bastards* (*Quel Maledetto Treno Blindato*, 1978), which was later revisited by Quentin Tarantino in 2009.

Williamson also interpreted roles in movies such as *The New Barbarians* (*I Nuovi Barbari*), *1990: The Bronx Warrior* (*1990: I guerrieri del Bronx*, Castellari 1982) and *Warrior of the Lost World* (*I Guerrieri dell'Anno 2072*, 1983) by Lucio Fulci, acquiring an important part also in the later genre of the Italian "post-atomic" movies, directly derived from the model of *Mad Max* (George Miller, 1979) and *Escape from New York* (*1997: Fuga da New York*, John Carpenter, 1981). This genre would represent the conclusion of the creative and productive golden age started with the Post-War reconstruction, Neorealism and *peplum*.

The memory of this forever-lost world that so deeply penetrated the imaginary fabric at an individual and collective level, resurfaces in one of the most beautiful and obscure stories in *Sillabario n. 2* by Goffredo Parise, published in 1982. The short story, entitled *Roma*, is focused from the very beginning on the weight that history and time exert on monuments in urban spaces, on inhabitants and on the protagonist himself returning home on a train: "A winter Sunday, in the twilight, a man who felt like a stranger, but wasn't, arrived with a fast train, from the North, to the Rome station. From the train, the first appearance of the city and of its huge houses grafted on the scruffy hills full of garbage and grease, then those stones of the Arch of Porta Maggiore packed with grass and little trees. He saw the violet and silky sky with the quiet and cold air of the north wind. He felt, as always when he was arriving, *the mortal presence of the centuries and of history.*"[13]

In this context, antiquity — juxtaposed, in the present, with the "scruffy hills full of garbage and grease" — is animated by new and, at the same time, archaic presences: Africans, who capture the protagonist's gaze. Their "savage and powerful" bearing activates a flux of remembrances, scholastic and cinematographic memories, classical scenes of the fall of the Roman Empire mediated by the movies seen by the author thirty years before: "So, the man could see Rome, after having lived there for so many years, as he had never seen it. The one he was seeing was populated by African men; there were some soldiers wrapped in their restless or confused canine solitude, continuous groups of Bedouin women in their white costumes with their little black legs, nervous and elderly, and tattooed crosses on their foreheads. Then men of different races, among which, beside the thermal baths of Diocletian, a group of tall, sinewy black men, with thin garments draped over muscles that appeared to have been oiled. They had shaved heads and walked in a savage and at the same time powerful way, which reminded the man of Nubian slaves, the flagellations in late-empire processions, the masseurs, the imposing and slippery attendants of the thermal baths. This impression, like that *from a scene in a movie transported into reality stayed with him forever*."[14]

So, the vivid presence of Africans is inserted within the "mortal presence of the centuries and of history": but for the Western eye this is the "impression of a movie scene transported into reality," a spontaneously realized *peplum*, concrete, and at the same time hallucinatory. This pervasive feeling invades the whole atmosphere of the description and of the narrative, haunting them, and remains with the protagonist. The cinematographic screen becomes a filter that combines collective and individual memories, dreams and transfigurations of reality: all these elements contribute to build a powerful scene portraying in an effective and non-didactic way an African Italian identity that during the Eighties was forming within the city and the rest of society, through increasing immigration and the birth of new generations of black Italians.

On the other hand for Parise Africa and its results constitute a well established memory in his own imaginative history: in 1968 he dedicated one of his famous narrative reportages to Biafra (both published in 1976 in *Guerre Lontane*), that articulated the issue of "distance," exotic even in its capacity to terrify, conveyed through a typically Italian perspective, that is, humanistic and open to the reality of the world (as in the case of Pasolini and Moravia, with whom he shares many key points). So, the observed scenes are activated and loaded with themes and ideas, which were meditated and elaborated for a long time (the "poor, essential nakedness"). Only a profoundly and authentically Italian writer like Parise could capture the mysterious and archaic gaze of children that he helplessly observes with a sort of admiration: "... seen together, one next to the other, they form a crowd of little old men, polite, calm, waiting in silence. No one moves towards me, no one stretches out his hand, no one asks anything, motivated by a last trembling of vitality, if by nothing else. From their poor, essential nakedness, on a terrain worn-out by their little bodies, they raise their eyes with difficulty, for an instant, then they look down again towards an empty place beside them: a look that is not sad, not desperate, not hungry, not scared, but calm and almost serene, detached, contemplative: of total and definitive intelligence of the things of this world, of the perfect comprehension of the solitude and pain of man. Two, three, five years old, this, for the most part, was how old they are, they nonetheless possess the greatness of those who have known and experienced the entire arc of a long life, and who are preparing to abandon it."[15]

In this silent encounter in a far away place, and in the narrative scene constructed fifteen years later skillfully combining the reality of the scene at the baths of Diocletian with precise and fantastic references to the cinematographic imagery of the economic "boom," we find one of the sources of the complex evolution of an identity fusing African and Italian characters, one that is still ongoing. All of which begins from the mysterious and precious points of contact that connect history to prehistory, antiquity to eternity.

[1] Statement of the director during the festival *Isola delle Storie*, Gavoi, 3 July 2011, during the celebrations for his eightieth birthday.

[2] This text was excerpted and translated from Pasolini, P.P., (1996). *Alì dagli occhi azzurri*. Milan: Garzanti, pp. 488-493, 515-516.

[3] *Ibid.*

[4] This text was excerpted and translated from Siciliano, E., (2005). *Vita di Pasolini*. Milan: Mondadori, p. 379.

[5] *Ibid.*, p. 378.

[6] *Ibid.*

[7] This text was excerpted and translated from Moravia, A., (2007). *A quale tribù appartieni?* Milan: Bompiani, p. 78. The book was first published in 1972.

[8] *Ibid.*, p. 76.

[9] *Ibid.*, p. 94.

[10] *Ibid.*, p. 15.

[11] This text was excerpted and translated from De Martino, E. (2011). *Sud e magia*. Milan: Feltrinelli, p. 95. The book was first published in 1959.

[12] Strode played also in Di Leo's *Colpo in canna* (1975).

[13] This text was excerpted and translated from Parise, G. (2013). *Roma*, in *Sillabari n. 2*. Milan: Adelphi, p. 329. The book was first published in 1982.

[14] *Ibid.*, pp. 330-331.

[15] This text was excerpted and translated from Parise, G. (2007) *Biafra*, in *Guerre politiche*. Milan: Adelphi, p. 112. The book was first published in 1976.

African Americans and Italy

Stanley Whitney
Primordial Color II, 1997
Oil on canvas
136×157 cm
Courtesy of Mauro Nicoletti

109

Terry Adkins
Greater Deeps (from Firmament RHA), 1995
Tin and wood
81×69×46 cm
Courtesy of the Estate of Terry Adkins

Lorna Simpson
Cloudscape (still images), 2004
Single channel video with sound
6 minutes duration, loop
Performer: Terry Adkins
Courtesy of the Artist

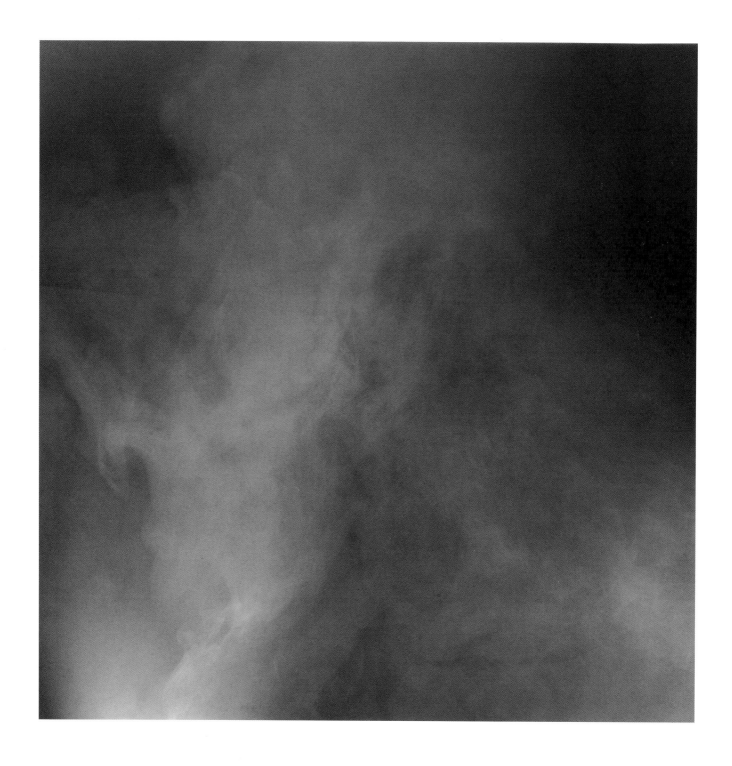

Elisabetta Benassi
Ships and Still More Ships, 2015
Watercolor on paper
40×60 cm
Courtesy of the Artist
and Magazzino, Rome

I ask that every member of the race give his moral and financial support to this convention.

The Universal Negro Improvement Association is now raising a fund of Two Million Dollars, and it is expecting that every Negro will give from one to one hundred dollars contribution to this fund. You can do so by sending your donation addressed to the Chancellor of the Universal Negro Improvement Association, 54-56 West 135th street, New York City U. S. A.

The Black Star Line Steamship Corporation requests the support of all Negroes. The slogan of the corporation at this time is "SHIPS AND STILL MORE SHIPS," and it is now the intention of the directors to purchase and build ships of larger tonnage for the African and South American trade, therefore it is up to every member of the race to do his and her bit in buying more shares in this progressive corporation. The shares are still going at Five Dollars each, and you may buy from one to two hundred shares.

$2,000,000 Convention

Garvey July, 3 20
N York

Elisabetta Benassi
Ships and Still More Ships, 2015
Flyer
26×15 cm
Courtesy of the Artist
and Magazzino, Rome

THE NEGRO IN THE REALM OF COMMERCE

Every Negro Should Buy Stocks
in the

BLACK STAR LINE STEAMSHIP CORPORATION

Capitalized at $500,000, Under the Laws of the State of Delaware, United States of America

A LINE OF STEAMSHIPS TO RUN BETWEEN AMERICA, AFRICA, THE WEST INDIES, CANADA, SOUTH AND CENTRAL AMERICA, CARRYING FREIGHT AND PASSENGERS

THE BLACK STAR LINE Will Open Up Untold Possibilities for the Race. Stocks Sold Only to Negroes

---

You Can Buy From One to Two Hundred Shares at $5.00 Each

Buy Now! Call or Write the Main Office

Black Star Line, Inc.

56 WEST 135th STREET

New York City, New York, U. S. A.

Claudia Durastanti
Black and White (Don't) Make Gray

I moved to Torpignattara in 2009, when there was almost no street art to take pictures of and riots and deaths didn't make the national news; the neighborhood was just another circle in the stifling Pasolinian myth. I had no sympathy for those who hung out there trying to channel him; he had been dead for a while.

I didn't move into Torpignattara naively; I pursued it. I wanted to be in Rome where it didn't feel like Rome. Plus, it reminded me of southern parts of Brooklyn in the Nineties, where Chinese and Russians had overwhelmed Italians without visible bloodshed. I moved in during the summer, getting accustomed to loud Far East dance tunes seeping through my windows, men leaning over their cars or chilling on their grocery store steps until two in the morning. It did feel like some Brooklyn I had known: dirty, crowded and mostly unaware.

The first people I talked to in the neighborhood were quite different, but ended up saying the same thing. The first was the female owner of a tiny pizza place. She was complaining about the lack of business and believed it was mostly the *others'* fault. The others being, I supposed, the Bengali — the largest community in the neighborhood — and Arabs who opened kebab shops and eventually learned how to make pizza. She was one of the few ladies who still baked on her own, unwilling to hire foreigners for help.

The second person was the owner of the Indian restaurant in front of my apartment, Aziz. By stating his name and not the woman's, I'm not suggesting we were more likely to become friends in name of a shared experience of strangeness, but the lady never introduced herself in three years, even though I was a regular client. Which proves what I had thought from the beginning: she was not a racist, she was just grumpy. And if I had to label her as a xenophobe, I would have said she was a cloudy one, like many people in the neighborhood, with undistinguished and moody outbursts of discomfort vanishing away more quickly than not.

Aziz wished and hoped and longed for a more domestic audience; he played along but resented it when his place was seen as *exotic*. He wanted a regular clientele, not just bohemians or compatriots. "That's not where my money is going to come from." *Locals* were his others, and they weren't helping the business.

I remember laughing at that: a working class neighborhood subject to endless migration waves slowly going artsy; were we really talking about otherness and exoticism in 2009? But that was Rome. Everywhere else there would have been luxury condos, fully booked real estate agents, gallery openings, buttery overcrowded Sunday brunches. Except Torpignattara is no Hackney, no Belleville, no Bed-Stuy and yet it's not some banlieue on fire. Occasionally, Roman friends who had never been in the area would ask if they needed a *permesso di soggiorno* (a residence permit) to visit and made me smile by calling it a *periferia* (outskirts): it took me only twenty minutes to reach the city center by public transportation.

People tend to say that Esquilino — the area behind Termini Station usually referred to as Rome's Chinatown — and Torpignattara are similar, but I always thought the former was more mysterious and opaque. Maybe it's because of the arcades surrounding Piazza Vittorio, while Torpignattara's high street and open sizable alleys make it more exposed: urban planning is not encouraging any particular brand of seediness here. What these two neighborhoods have in common is the fact they ended up being *a touch of color in Rome* in the Lonely Planet sense, without the amount of comfort that usually comes with it.

An article in *Blow Up* featuring some noise bands scattered or interested in the area known as *Borgata Boredom — Music and Noises from Roma Est* called Via di Torpignattara "the Fifth Avenue of Islamabad." I remember being puzzled by the remark: did it mean it was a fancy street in a land of ruins? I know nothing about Islamabad, but I imagine it as a place with less ethnic or demographic variety than the one Torpignattara currently displays, which is enough to make it more interesting. To me, the high street was this bizarre hybrid between a Roman townesque neighborhood, a *borgata*, and an Asian capital, yes, but the more I lived there, the less I had the urge to compare it to a foreign city to hype it up. Torpignattara was its own thing. But if the definition diverted attention from crime rates, maybe it was a good sign. Things were moving forward. Kicking in.

I moved out of Torpignattara after three years, but I recently paid a visit. I had heard about the giant murals covering some of its buildings, so I expected to see some changes. Several street artists, including the duo Etam Cru, Sten Lex, Ludo and Jacopo Ceccarelli, were invited by the City Culture Council and the association Wunderkammern to contribute to a project called *Light Up Torpigna!* The idea was to put Torpignattara on the map of street art as the neighborhood was having a hard time,

following the accidents related to racial and political issues openly exploited by right wing movements this last fall.

No matter the pressure of Conrad mythomaniacs expecting to visit Rome's heart of darkness, I never witnessed a crime or particular mischief in the area when I lived there. People asked me if I had heard about the two Chinese girls buried in a wall or the latest money laundering scam, but it all ended up sounding like a hard-boiled novel set in a city that needed to get its act together, given that immigration was hardly a sudden emergency.

All kinds of things were happening: I remember people throwing chairs at each other near a flower shop over a long summer night, everybody hysterical from the heat; men drinking cough medicine on the post office steps next to the local mosque in a throwback to Eighties drug culture, but that made the area more bizarre than dangerous.

I'm not suggesting everything was pretty: when local resident Stefano Cucchi died after being brutalized by the police and neglected by doctors, people setting trash bins on fire under my window were mostly white like the victim; solidarity and grief were narrower than they could have been. When Khan Muhamad Shanzad — a 28-year-old Pakistani — was killed on the sidewalk by a neighbor ten years his junior last September, there were counter-demonstrations against anti-racism appeals in the streets. It seemed to me that people in Torpignattara had this kind of implicit policy when it came to cohabitation: hit to get hit back.

A symmetrical dynamic, although with different strength, power and rights on each side.

I usually resist metaphors comparing a city to a human body. Cities evolve over time and migration is a brutalizing force due to which some blood spills here and some bones break there, but it's hard to adopt this evocative image when you live in that body and you can become the wound. At the same time, I came to think about Torpignattara as a kid after a fever, unsure what to do with the body that's left after all the stretching and sweating under the covers. A kid with larger limbs, awkward parts and whose voice has changed over night; a kid taking over, suddenly becoming stronger, cooler and luminescent. What confounded about the murals of *Light up Torpigna!* was the fact that they partially stood out as an effort to paint the sick kid's cast in cheery colors during the convalescence, while the patient preferred perhaps to paint his own thing, whether ugly or not.

There's an unpretentious mural in Torpignattara near the Acquedotto Alessandrino, which I came to appreciate over the years, although at first it gave me that Bob Geldof's Live Aid feel. It's a simple painting depicting typical inhabitants of the neighborhood and sealing a pact of intimacy with a bordering area, Il Quadraro. The wall is in a park where kids hang out after school — often with their moms — along with young couples and occasional hustlers. Maybe it's because of the location, but I always perceived it as a tribute to fragile alliances, like the ones mothers would establish while talking about their sons and daughters being bullied at school, and the villain was a villain regardless of nationality.

Because that's the case in Torpignattara: what nationality are you going to discuss anyway? Of 176 kids enrolled at the local Carlo Pisacane primary school — alternatively described as a national success or desolate failure, a vivacious example of integration or a wasteland slowly deserted by "official Italians" — only forty had Italian citizenship. Almost all of them were born here. Black and white don't necessarily make grey. But if there's one area in Rome where that could happen — even only for demographical unpoetic reasons — it's Torpignattara.

Aziz was one of the first people to call me when I moved to London. He wanted to promote his new shop closer to Pigneto; he no longer served that much Indian food and converted to baking pizza. I think I understood him, and that he had given up in a way, but not totally.

Like many acquaintances I had left in the neighborhood he made me think about pareidolia, a physiological phenomenon according to which we perceive patterns in random or meaningless data, like when we see animals in clouds or faces in a moldy piece of wall. In a way, pareidolia can be considered a particularly elegant cognitive disorder. Walking in Torpignattara, I often experience precisely that. I think I recognize a city, Rome, or at least how it should be by now. I'm not sure it's there, and most won't agree, but I see it.

Immigration/Integration

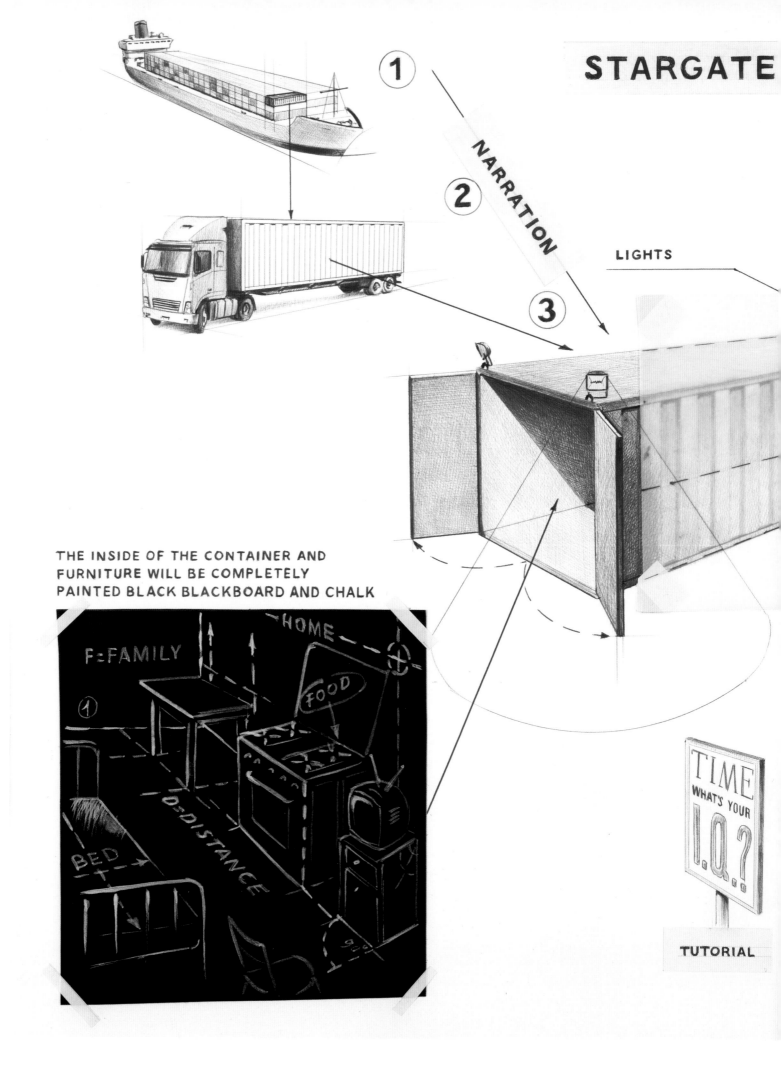

NARRATION

1
2
3

LIGHTS

THE INSIDE OF THE CONTAINER AND
FURNITURE WILL BE COMPLETELY
PAINTED BLACK BLACKBOARD AND CHALK

F=FAMILY

HOME

FOOD

D=DISTANCE

BED

TIME
WHAT'S YOUR
I.Q.?

TUTORIAL

ENTRANCE

NARRATION

DOLBY SURROUND SYSTEM

RECORDED CONVERSATION
BETWEEN EMIGRANTS AND
PLACE OF ORIGIN

CALL CENTER

COMMUNICATION

EMIGRANTS

PLACE OF ORIGIN

ROME

Giuseppe Stampone
Stargate, 2015
Site-specific installation
Container, software, dolby
stereo S.7.0, painting,
blackboard and acrylic
6×3 m
Courtesy of the Artist

Pietro Ruffo
Mar di Sicilia, 2015
Watercolor and cut paper
35×50 cm
Courtesy of Galleria Lorcan O'Neill, Rome

Pietro Ruffo
Mar di Sicilia, 2015
Watercolor and cut paper
35×50 cm
Courtesy of Galleria Lorcan O'Neill, Rome

Francesco Arena
Passi, 2015
Bronze, 2 pieces
68×10×10 cm
Courtesy of the Artist
and Galleria Raffaella Cortese, Milan

Emily Jacir
stazione, 2008-2009
Public installation on Line 1 Vaporetto stops:
Ca' D'Oro, S. Zaccaria and Rialto Mercato
Digital C-prints
Dimensions variable
Courtesy of the Artist

Do Italian Men Love
Black Women?
Taiye Selasi

In 2011 I came to Rome intending to stay for weeks. Within a day I decided to relocate from New York. I'd fallen rather hopelessly in love with the city's beauty: the pastel palette, the sky, the light. But no one seemed to believe me. Without exception, acquaintances would ask, "Did you move to Rome for a man?", adding with a cheerful wink, "Italian men love black women."

Italian men love black women.

Raised by my Nigerian mum in Boston, I cannot remember meeting an Italian of any gender until my early twenties. Still, long before I moved to Rome I heard the adage uttered as truth: by West African aunties, African American girlfriends, magazines, films. In college my best friend, reared like me in predominantly white American suburbs, spent a semester studying in Florence. It was, she insisted, the first time that she'd ever felt so desirable, irresistible as she was to Italian men.

But I didn't believe her. As a rule, I reject such generalizations, painfully aware of how easily they obscure the humanity of those they describe. To my mind "Italian men" was as unpromising a way to begin a thoughtful sentence as "Africans" or "black people," the slots into which I am often shoved. I arrived in Italy prepared to dismiss a decade's worth of anecdote, certain that the claims of national negrophilia were overblown.

I was wrong. In my fairly extensive travels I have never experienced anything quite like walking through the streets of Rome as a brown-skinned woman. I was shocked by the intensity of the attention, the exultant references to my skin, the vocal preference of many men for black women over, say, blond. If *all* (heterosexual) Italian men

could not be said to love black women, the perception shared a border with reality. Somewhere within the fabric of Italian culture lay an obsession with the brown female body, palpable to me as a brown-skinned woman.

Nowhere was the nature of this fetish more apparent than in the narrative of Karima El Mahroug. In January 2011 I arrived in Rome speaking no Italian; as one does, I "listened to" the television to learn. The Ruby Rubacuori scandal, then, introduced me to both the language and the shame of my new home. The portrayals of Berlusconi's relationship with the North African adolescent smacked of classic racist iconography: the Africanized "bunga bunga" rite, the hypersexualized brown woman, the powerful white male savior. There was something surreal about the display: twenty-first century journalists spewing eighteenth century bigotry without embarrassment, without reproach. Soon my question was not *whether* a racial fetish could be said to exist in Italy but rather *how* it flourished alongside such flagrantly racist thought.

In 2013 a headline in *The Guardian* posed a question I'd asked often since relocating: "Why is Italy still so racist?" Citing the verbal abuse of footballers Kévin Constant and Kevin-Prince Boateng, the bananas hurled at Cécile Kyenge, Berlusconi's quip about Obama's "suntan," the article explores the roots of Italian racism. In two years in Rome I'd begun to hear the phrase "Italy is racist" as frequently, and uttered as unwaveringly, as "Italian men love black women." In both cases the question of interest for me was not to what extent the generalizations were true — of course, *all* Italians don't [fill in the blank] — but what sociocultural dynamics, what manifest systems of thought had led to the claims?

It is easy enough to dismiss as ignorant the individual who hurls fruit at an elected official, to decry the drunken fan who chants slurs at a football match. It is harder and more important to understand the context in which such actions become possible, the unspoken agreements of the society that accepts such actions without prohibitive uproar. There is the man who makes the racist joke and there is the audience who laughs. To consider how racism actually works one must investigate the logic that informs the tendencies of the joker *and* the tolerance of his peers. Among possible explanations for both — joker and peer — *The Guardian* lists: "the legacy of Fascism and the continuing adulation of Benito Mussolini; the tangible insecurity, even sense of inferiority, of many Italians; widespread economic misery for at least the last decade; and a political class that is absurdly ignorant." I would suggest that, taken together, these influences inform a collective logic under which the African Other is disaggregated into intolerable and tolerable figures.

Rather, *figure*. The single tolerable African figure in Italian society is the inherently sexualized, fundamentally disempowered woman. Who else? The African footballer, possessing both physical and economic power, is demeaned. The African politician, possessing both political and intellectual power, is denigrated. The male African immigrant, selling handbags on street corners or left to die off the coast of Lampedusa, is demonized. His (imagined) power lies in his (alleged) intention to commit crimes, to seduce white Italian women, to steal white Italians' jobs. The non-sexualized African woman (the Ghanaian *badante*, the veiled Somali) is dismissed. If power threatens, powerlessness repels — unless, of course, it is sequined with sex. I chanced to attend a few of the parties *La Grande Bellezza* so brilliantly depicts, wildly indulgent gatherings of the Roman upper class. At each I found, unfailingly, some impossibly gorgeous African woman dressed in impossibly high stiltettos, accompanying an Italian man. There were no African men at these fetes, no African women intellectuals; my presence baffled everyone, bejeweled African women included. I was not a thing for which Italian society had a place. I was not the ideal African woman. The ideal African woman is both sexually potent and socially vulnerable, desperately in need of her Italian lover's approval and/or patronage. In possessing her, his *facetta nera*, the Italian man becomes both seducer and savior, expressing precisely the dominance denied him on the global stage.

In 2015 I left Rome, weary of attention. The Italian translation of my novel had reached the Top 10 on Amazon.it — but I had never felt so invisible, irresistible as I was to Italian men. The attention told a story: you are a sexually attractive African woman, your novel doesn't much matter, your intelligence is incidental. Of course, no one said this. Of course, many readers attended seriously to the book. Of course, I count among my friends the most thoughtful of Italian men (and women). Of course. But to live in a culture is to experience, daily, its assumptions. Is to know oneself both as one is and as one is seen, and unseen. Desire is not why I came to Rome, but might be why I left it.

Persistent Stereotypes

Adam Broomberg & Oliver Chanarin
Untitled (Scarti 40), 2013
Twice-printed lithographic paper
18.8×23.9 cm
Trolley Books, 2003
Courtesy of the Hiscox Collection

Adam Broomberg & Oliver Chanarin
Untitled (Scarti 33), 2013
Twice-printed lithographic paper
18.5×24.7 cm
Trolley Books, 2003
Courtesy of the Hiscox Collection

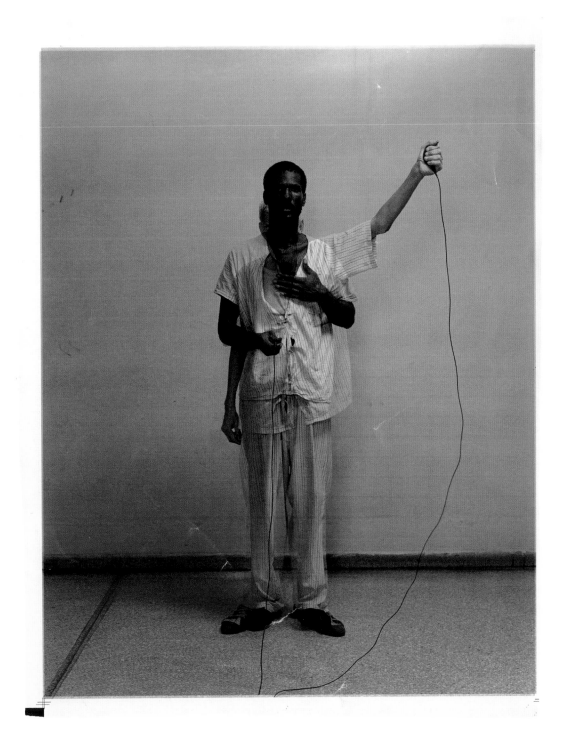

Adam Broomberg & Oliver Chanarin
Untitled (Scarti 4), 2013
Twice-printed lithographic paper
19.4×24.8 cm
Trolley Books, 2003
Courtesy of the Hiscox Collection

Adam Broomberg & Oliver Chanarin
Untitled (Scarti 26), 2013
Twice-printed lithographic paper
18.6×24 cm
Trolley Books, 2003
Courtesy of the Hiscox Collection

Invernomuto
Morositas, 2015
Collage, *from Malù - Lo stereotipo
della Venere Nera in Italia*
Video
Courtesy of the Artists

Jebila Okongwu
*The Economics of Reality
is my Nationality*, 2015
Installation (detail). Archivally
treated banana boxes, fishing line,
polyurethane foam and hot glue
Dimensions variable
Courtesy of the Artist

Lyle Ashton Harris
Untitled (Thuram), 2001
Black and white silver gelatin print
Image size 40×27.5 cm, paper size 50×41 cm
Edition of 10
Courtesy of the Artist
and Jablonka Maruani Mercier Gallery,
Brussels and Knokke

Lyle Ashton Harris
Verona #2, 2001
Black and white silver gelatin print
Image size 40×27.5 cm, paper size 50×41 cm
Edition of 10
Courtesy of the Artist
and Jablonka Maruani Mercier Gallery,
Brussels and Knokke

Lyle Ashton Harris
Roman Stranger # 7, 2001
Black and white silver gelatin print
Image size 40×27.5 cm, paper size 50×41 cm
Edition of 10
Courtesy of the Artist
and Jablonka Maruani Mercier Gallery,
Brussels and Knokke

Nari Ward
Staller, 2013
Reinforcement steel bars,
hammock, concrete
235×140×80 cm
Courtesy of Galleria Continua,
San Gimignano, Beijing, Les Moulins

Biographies

Terry Adkins (1953, Washington D.C. — 2014, New York, USA), a recipient of the Rome Prize at the American Academy in Rome in 2009, was an installation artist, musician, activist, cultural practitioner and Professor of Fine Art at the University of Pennsylvania. Influenced by "assemblage" artists, Adkins created sculpture from discarded objects. His references are the cultural tradition of the African American South, including crafts, trades, music, and folklore. He often reinserted historically transformative figures to their rightful place in the landscape of regional and world history. Exhibitions of his work were held at, among other places, Skidmore College, the American Academy in Rome, the Institute of Contemporary Art, University of Pennsylvania, and the Smithsonian Institution, Washington, D.C. His works are part of several collections, including those of the Museum of Modern Art and the Metropolitan Museum of Art in New York, the Hirshhorn Museum and Sculpture Garden in Washington, D.C.

Francesco Arena (1978, Mesagne, Italy), lives and works in Cassano delle Murge, Bari. His abstract, conceptual works involve a wide range of materials, but are united in their aim to re-present and scrutinize past events, often those associated with contemporary Italian history. Arena's primary subjects are occurrences of trauma, violence, and struggle, and their manifestation as statistical facts and in narratives and in collective memory. Topics addressed in previous works have included the clandestine escape of migrants, political assassinations, World War II bombings, accidental deaths of criminals, and large-scale massacres. He was among the artists chosen to represent Italy at the 55th Venice Biennale.

Bridget Baker (1971, East London, South Africa) lives and works in London and Cape Town. Her work intertwines documentary and memory-construction, forming a series of complex visual fragments realized through filmmaking, installation and performed re-stagings. Her practice and visual language, while based on in-depth research into questions about her own past, as well as collective memory within colonial and postcolonial narratives, remains speculative, nomadic and disquieting. She has produced work for various solo presentations, including The National Arts Festival in Grahamstown, Centro des Artes Contemporanea in Burgos, The Wapping Project and MAMbo. Her works have been included in numerous South African and international group exhibitions. Her films have also been included in *Recontres Internationales* at the Gaîté Lyrique, the 57th International Short Film Competition in Oberhausen, the Glasgow Short Film Festival and the Found Footage Film Festival.

Elisabetta Benassi (1966, Rome, Italy) makes reference in her work to the cultural, political and artistic traditions of the twentieth century, including psychoanalysis and other controversial themes. She uses various media (installation, photography, video) as devices in emotionally engaging work that shifts the moral focus onto the viewer. The results question contemporary identity and the human condition more broadly in relation to history. She participated in the 54th and 55th Venice Biennales and she is featured in *Personne et les Autres,* the Belgian Pavilion at this year's 56th Venice Biennale. She has also presented her work in solo shows at Gallery Jousse Entreprise, CRAC Alsace, Fondazione Merz and Magazzino, Rome. Her work was included in the exhibitions *Mutatis Mutandis*, Wiener Secession, Vienna, Austria and *Newtopia: The State of Human Rights*, Mechelen, Belgium.

Adam Broomberg (1970, Johannesburg, South Africa) **& Oliver Chanarin** (1971, London, UK) live and work in London. Tackling politics, race, religion, war and history, Broomberg & Chanarin prise open the fault lines associated with such imagery, creating new ways of understanding the human condition. Through painstaking restitution of found objects or imagery, Broomberg & Chanarin enact an archeology or exorcism of aesthetic and ideological constructs behind the accepted tropes of visual culture. They have had numerous international exhibitions including those at the Museum of Modern Art, Tate Britain, Tate Liverpool, the Gwangju Biennale, the Stedelijk Museum, the International Center of Photography, KW Institute for Contemporary Art, Mathaf Arab Museum of Modern Art and Museo Jumex. Their work is represented in major public and private collections including Tate Modern, the Museum of Modern Art, the Stedelijk Museum, the Victoria and Albert Museum, the Musée de l'Elysée, the International Center of Photography, and the Art Gallery of Ontario.

Christian Caliandro (1979, Mottola, Italy) is an art historian and curator based in Bari. He is the author of numerous articles and books in the field of cultural politics, including *La trasformazione delle immagini. L'inizio del postmoderno tra arte, cinema e teoria, 1977-1983* (Mondadori Electa, 2008) and, with Pier Luigi Sacco, *Italia Reloaded. Ripartire con la Cultura* (Il Mulino, 2011). In 2013, he published *Italia Revolution. Ri-*

nascere con la Cultura (Bompiani). He contributes frequently to the culture pages of several periodicals, including *Artribune* and the *Corriere del Mezzogiorno-Corriere della Sera.*

Alessadro Ceresoli (1975, Romano di Lombardia, Italy) investigates the creative act, as well as the subject and its individuality; his drawings, which allegorize process, form the core of his research around which he develops various related projects. In them, the excess of forms and signs creates a sort of stratification of information. Images and thoughts pile up and aspire to a monochrome appearance, which is undermined by a volatile and unstable surface. Selected exhibitions include a solo outing at the Castello Sforzesco and group shows at Andrew Mummery Gallery, carlier / gebauer, Villa delle Rose, Macro — Museo Arte Contemporanea in Rome and Fondazione Sandretto Re Rebaudengo.

Barbara Chase-Riboud (1939, Philadelphia, PA, USA) is an internationally acclaimed visual artist, novelist and poet, who lives between Rome and Paris. She is best known for her 1979 historical novel *Sally Hemings*. She received her Bachelor of Arts from the Tyler School at Temple University in 1957. In the same year, she was awarded the John Hay Whitney fellowship to study at the American Academy

in Rome for twelve months, the first African American woman to receive that honor. During her year in Rome, she made her first sculptures in bronze. In the late 1960s, she began making large sculptures combining cast-bronze abstract shapes with fiber ropes braided from silk and wool. In 1996, Chase-Riboud was among the artists commissioned to contribute to the African Burial Ground National Monument at the federal courthouse in Lower Manhattan; her memorial, *Africa Rising*, was installed in 1998. Her *Malcom X Steles*, which reinvent the traditional depiction of the figure in post-World War II European Art, were exhibited at the Philadelphia Museum of Art and the Berkeley Museum in 2013-2014 as part of a major survey of work created between 1969 and 2008. In 1996, she was awarded the *Chevalier des Arts et des Lettres* from the French Government. She is represented in several major collections, including those of the Metropolitan Museum of Art in New York and the Centre Pompidou in Paris.

Onyedika Chuke (Onitsha, Nigeria) graduated in 2011 from the Cooper Union in New York, where he continues to live and work. His ongoing project, *The Forever Museum*, analyzes the historiography of museum objects, exploring the relationship between these objects and history, transforming them in order to examine disjunctures between historical artifacts, architecture, politics and the human body. Chuke has completed a number of residencies and commissions, including the Bronx Museum of the Arts' AIM program and the Verbier Public Art Commission in Switzerland. He is the 2013 Van Lier Visual Art Fellow at Wave Hill Public Garden and Cultural Center, as well as a recipient of a New York City public art commission on Randall's Island, completed in the summer of 2014.

Claudia Durastanti (1984, Brooklyn, USA) is a journalist and writer currently living in London. Her debut novel, *Un giorno verrò a lanciare sassi alla tua finestra* (Marsilio, 2010) was awarded the Premio Castiglioncello Opera Prima and the Premio Mondello Giovani. Her second novel, *A Chloe, per le ragioni sbagliate*, also published by Marsilio, appeared in 2013. In 2015, she was the Italian Affiliated Fellow in Literature at the American Academy in Rome.

Theo Eshetu (1958, London, UK) grew up in Addis Ababa, Dakar, and Belgrade, before settling in Rome. Focusing on video's expressive potential and his exploration of African cultures, Eshetu explores perception, culture, and notions of the sacred through electronic time-based media and optical devices and effects. He draws from anthropology, art history, scientific research and religion to explore clashes and harmonies of human subjectivity between world cultures in the global context. His work has appeared at The New Museum, the New York African Film Festival, DIA Foundation's Electronic Arts Intermix, the International Center for Photography, the Baltimore Museum of Art; the Smithsonian National Museum of African Art, the ICA, the Hayward Gallery; as well as at the Venice Film Festival, Roma Film Festival, Museum of Modern and Contemporary Art in Nice, the UNESCO headquarters in Paris and the Martin Gropius Bau in Berlin.

Lyle Ashton Harris (1965, New York, USA) is a Trustee of the American Academy in Rome and Associate Professor at New York University. He received the Rome Prize at the American Academy in Rome in 2001. He has cultivated a diverse artistic practice, ranging from photographic media, collage, installation and performance, to explore the impact of desire, ethnicity, and gender in the contemporary social and cultural dynamic. His work has been exhibited internationally, including at the 52nd Venice Biennale and is included in the collections of the Museum of Modern Art in New York, the Whitney Museum of American Art, the Solomon R. Guggenheim Museum, the Museum of Contemporary Art, Los Angeles, the Los Angeles County Museum of Art, and the Museo de Arte Contemporáneo de Castilla y León (MUSAC).

Simone Bertuzzi (1983, Piacenza, Italy) and **Simone Trabucchi** (1982, Piacenza, Italy) have been collaborating as **Invernomuto** since 2003. Although they primarily work in moving image and sound, Invernomuto also integrate sculpture, publishing, and performance in their practice. Recent solo exhibitions of their work have been held at the Triennale di Milano (*Anabasis Articulata*), Marsèlleria, Milan, Museion and ar/ge kunst, Bolzano, GAMeC, Bergamo, Padiglione d'Arte Contemporanea, Ferrara, Grimmuseum, Berlin. In 2013 Invernomuto was a finalist in the nineth edition of the *Premio Furla* and they won the first edition of the MERU ART*SCIENCE Award. Bertuzzi and Trabucchi also pursue individual practices in the field of music, performing under the names Palm Wine and Dracula Lewis, respectively.

Palestinian artist and filmmaker **Emily Jacir** (1970, Bethlehem, West Bank) spent her childhood in Saudi Arabia, and attended high school in Italy. She currently divides her time between Rome and Ramallah. Her work spans a diverse range of media and strategies including film, photography, social interventions, installation, performance, video, writing and sound. Jacir has shown extensively throughout Europe, the Americas and the Middle East since 1994. Solo exhibitions include Whitechapel Gallery, Darat al Funun in Amman, Beirut Art Center, Guggenheim Museum and Kunstmuseum St. Gallen. Jacir participated in dOCUMENTA (13), the 51st, 52nd and 53rd Venice Biennales, 15th Biennale of Sydney, Sharjah Biennial 7 and the 8th Istanbul Biennial. Awards include, among others, a Golden Lion at the 52nd Venice Biennale and the Guggenheim Museum Hugo Boss Prize.

Italian writer **Vincenzo Latronico** (1984, Rome, Italy) received his degree in philosophy from the Università degli Studi in Milan. His debut novel, *Ginnastica e Rivoluzione*, was published by Bompiani in 2008, followed by *La cospirazione delle colombe*, also published by Bompiani, in 2011. English publications include *Remedies to the absence of Reiner Ruthenbeck* (Archive Books, 2011) and *Criticism as fiction?* (Kaleidoscope Press, 2011). *Narciso nelle colonie. Un altro viaggio in Etiopia*, his collaboration with Armin Linke excerpted in these pages, was published by Quodlibet Humboldt in 2011.

Armin Linke (1966, Milan, Italy) lives and works in Milan and Berlin. As a photographer and filmmaker he combines a range of contemporary image-processing technologies in order to blur the borders between fiction and reality. His artistic practice is concerned with different possibilities of dealing with photographic archives and their respective manifestations, as well as with the interrelations and transformative powers between urban, architectural or spatial functions and the human beings interacting with these environments. Through work with his own archive, as well as with other historical archives, Linke challenges the conventions of photographic practice, whereby the questions of how photography is installed and displayed become increasingly important. Linke is currently professor at the HfG Karlsruhe. Recent solo exhibitions include *Armin Linke/Alpi* at the Voralburger Architektur Institut, in Dornbirn, Austria; *Inside/Outside*, at Sciences Po - Bibliothèque René Redmond, Paris; and *Corpo dello Stato*, MAXXI, Rome.

Peter Benson Miller (1968, New York, USA), an art historian and curator, is Andrew Heiskell Arts Director at the American Academy in Rome. In 2010, he curated the exhibition *Philip Guston, Roma* at the Museo Carlo Bilotti — Aranciera di Villa Borghese in Rome, which then traveled to the Phillips Collection in Washington, D.C. *Go Figure! New Perspectives on Guston*, which he edited, was published by New York Review Books and the American Academy in Rome in 2015.

Meleko Mokgosi (1981, Francistown, Botswana) works within an interdisciplinary framework to create large-scale project-based installations that combine and reconfigure history painting, cinematic tropes, psychoanalysis, and post-colonial theory. He interrogates narrative formulas and the fundamental models for the inscription and transmission of history alongside established European notions of representation in order to address questions of nationhood, anti-colonial sentiments, and the perception of historicized events. His work has been exhibited nationally and internationally at venues including the Botswana National Gallery, The Hudson Valley Center for Contemporary Art Museum, The Studio Museum in Harlem, the Armand Hammer Museum of Art and Culture Center in Los Angeles, Yerba Buena Center for the Arts, the Lyon Museum of Contemporary Art and the Institute of Contemporary Art in Boston.

Jebila Okongwu (1975, London, UK), the son of an Australian mother with Scottish ancestry and a Nigerian father, was raised in Africa and Australia before moving to Rome, where he has lived and worked for over a decade. His work in various media, including sculpture, performance and painting, draws upon motifs reminiscent of his African heritage, namely the geometrical carving characteristic of tribal art from his father's native eastern Nigeria. He translates them into forms and objects made predominantly with colorful cardboard boxes for transporting bananas emblazoned with the logos of European fruit importers. He thus playfully sends up neo-colonial trade networks, the appropriations of Pop Art, as well as persistent racist and sexual stereotypes associated with the exotic other. His work has been featured in several solo and group shows in Italy, the United Kingdom, Australia and New York.

Senam Okudzeto (1972, Chicago, USA) is a transnational artist, writer, and scholar. She grew up in Ghana, Nigeria, the United Kingdom, and the United States, and she now divides her time between projects in Basel, London, New York, and Accra. Employing installation and collage elements drawing on personal biography, her work argues that national boundaries are constructed outside national boundaries as much as they are within. Okudzeto has taught in Europe, the USA, and West Africa and has received numerous awards and

fellowships, including the artist-in-residence program at the Studio Museum in Harlem, a Pollock-Krasner award and the Stiftung Laurenz Haus residency in Basel. Her work is included in the collections of several important public institutions, including the Amistaad Center in New Orleans, the Schaulager in Basel, and the Radcliffe Institute for Advanced Study at Harvard University.

Mark Robbins (New York, USA) an artist, curator and educator, is President of the American Academy in Rome. He has also served as the Executive Director of the International Center of Photography in New York, the Dean of the School of Architecture at Syracuse University, Director of Design at the National Endowment for the Arts, and the first Curator of Architecture at the Wexner Center for the Arts in Columbus, Ohio. He is the author of several books, including *American City X* (2014), *New Public Works* (2013), *Households* (2006) and *Angles of Incidence* (1992). Among his numerous awards are the Rome Prize and a fellowship from the Radcliffe Institute for Advanced Study at Harvard University.

Pietro Ruffo (1978, Rome, Italy), a visual artist, was trained as an architect at the Università Roma Tre. His analysis of contemporary history and strains

of political thought in complex installations and works on paper often echo and problematize the tools and modes of expression used by geographers, social scientists, philosophers and naturalists. The recipient of the *Premio New York*, and numerous artist residencies, his work has been the subject of a number of solo exhibitions, including those at the Fondazione Pastificio Cerere in Rome, the Centro Arti Visive Pescheria in Pesaro and the All Russian Museum of Decorative Applied and Folk Art in Moscow, among others. His work is part of several prominent public and private collections, including that of the MAXXI in Rome.

Taiye Selasi (1979, London, UK) is a writer and photographer of Nigerian and Ghanaian origin. She is the author of "Bye-Bye, Babar (Or: What is an Afropolitan)," first published in 2005, a seminal article defining an Afropolitan identity, sensibility and experience, and "The Sex Lives of African Girls, which appeared in *Granta* in 2011. Her novel *Ghana Must Go* was published to wide critical acclaim in 2013.

Lorna Simpson (1960, New York, USA) received her BFA in Photography from the School of Visual Arts in New York and her MFA from the University of California, San Diego. By the time she finished the graduate program at San Diego in 1985, she was already considered a pioneer of conceptual photography. In the same period, Simpson became well-known for her large-scale photograph and text works that confront and challenge narrow, conventional views of gender, identity, culture, history and memory. Her work has been exhibited at the Museum of Modern Art, New York; the Museum of Contemporary Art, Chicago; the Walker Art Center, Minneapolis; and the Irish Museum of Modern Art, Dublin, among other prestigious institutions. A recent retrospective, accompanied by a major publication, premiered recently at the Jeu de Paume in Paris, and traveled to the Haus der Kunst in Munich and the BALTIC Centre for Contemporary Art in Gateshead, England.

Frank M. Snowden, III (1946, Washington, D.C. USA) received his Ph.D. from Oxford University in 1975. His books include *Violence and Great Estates in the South of Italy: Apulia, 1900-1922* (1984); *The Fascist Revolution in Tuscany, 1919-1922* (1989); *Naples in the Time of Cholera* (1995), and *The Conquest of Malaria: Italy, 1900-1962* (2006), which was awarded the Gustav Ranis Prize from the MacMillan Center at Yale in 2007 as "the best book on an international topic by a member of the Yale Faculty;" the Helen and Howard R. Marraro Prize by the American Historical Association as the best work on Italy in any period; and the 2008 Welch Medal from the American Association for the History of Medicine. Snowden is the Andrew Downey Orrick Professor of History & History of Medicine at Yale University and has served on the Board of Trustees of the American Academy in Rome since 2010.

Giuseppe Stampone (1974, Cluses, France) is an Italian artist based in Rome and New York. He was the Cy Twombly Italian Affiliated Fellow in the Visual Arts in 2013 at the American Academy in Rome. His works range from multimedia installations to drawings made with Bic pen, a technique that has become his personal trademark. His art is unabashedly a potent form of political protest; though works of art and community-based interventions, he invites audiences to reflect upon issues such as immigration, natural disasters and war. He is the founder of *Solstizio*, a project co-financed by the European Union, to support a range of collaborative artistic interventions developed in various countries across the globe. His work has been exhibited throughout Italy and abroad in International Art Biennials, Museums and Foundations including the 56th Venice Bienniale, 11th Havana Biennial, Liverpool Biennial in 2010, 14th and 15th Quadriennale di Roma, MIT Museum Boston, Gwangju Museum of Art Kunsthalle, Wilfredo Lam Contemporary Art Center Havana, MAXXI in Rome, Palazzo Reale in Milan, Cabaret Voltaire in Zürich, GAMeC — Gallery of Modern and Contemporary Art in Bergamo.

Robert Storr (1949, Portland, Maine, USA), an influential art critic and curator, is the Dean of the Yale University School of Art. He was the Director of the 2007 Venice Biennale, the first American to have that honor. Formerly the Curator and then Senior Curator in the Department of Painting and Sculpture at the Museum of Modern Art in New York (1990-2002), he is the author of numerous catalogues, articles and books, including volumes on, among others, Ad Reinhardt, Gerhard Richter, Philip Guston, Robert Ryman and Louise Bourgeois.

Justin Randolph Thompson (1979, Peekskill, New York, USA) is a sculptor and new media artist. He is a graduate of the University of Tennessee and American University, where he received his MFA. Living between Italy and the United States since 2001, he has exhibited internationally and participated in numerous residencies on both sides of the Atlantic. His work explores the historic implications of triumph, victory and ascension by re-contextualizing references from Roman antiquity and interweaving them with aspects of African American culture both past and present. Exploring cultural displacement or imposed hierarchies and adorning status symbols with hybrid connotations through a talismanic application of culturally specific materials, his work encompasses sculptural installation, performance, video and sound. Recent solo or two-person shows include those at Momenta Art Gallery in Brooklyn; Weil Gallery, Texas A&M, Corpus Christi, Texas; Villa Romana, Florence; and Blue Star Contemporary Art Center_Project Space in San Antonio, Texas. In 2013, he was awarded a Louis Comfort Tiffany Foundation Award.

Nari Ward (1963, St. Andrew, Jamaica) makes dramatic sculptural installations composed of systematically collected material from his urban neighborhood. By revealing the emotions suffused within found everyday objects, Ward's works examine issues surrounding race, poverty, and consumer culture. His work has been widely exhibited on an international level, with solo exhibitions at the Louisiana State University Museum of Art in Baton Rouge, Massachusetts Museum of Contemporary Art in North Adams, Institute of Visual Arts, Milwaukee and Walker Art Center in Minneapolis. He has taken part in important group exhibitions, including the Whitney Biennial, Prospect 1 and Documenta XI. Ward's work is represented in the collections of numerous museums, including the Museum of Modern Art, Baltimore Museum of Art, Brooklyn Museum, the Walker Art Center and the Whitney Museum of American Art.

Carrie Mae Weems (1953, Portland, Oregon, USA) uses colloquial forms — jokes, songs, rebukes — in photographic series that scrutinize subjectivity and expose pernicious stereotypes. Weems's vibrant explorations of photography, video, and verse breathe new life into traditional narrative forms: social documentary, tableaux, self-portrait, and oral history. Eliciting epic contexts from individually framed moments, Weems debunks racist and sexist labels, examines the relationship between power and aesthetics, and uses personal biography to articulate broader truths. She traces an indirect history of the depiction of African Americans of more than a century. She has received honorary degrees from Colgate University and California College of the Arts. Weems's work has appeared in major exhibitions at Savannah College of Art and Design, W. E. B. Du Bois Institute for African and African American Research, Harvard University and Whitney Museum, among others.

Stanley Whitney (1946, Philadelphia, USA) draws upon his African American heritage, among other sources, to organize blocks of color into grids that fill the canvas, creating rhythmic and expressive structures infused by jazz music and reminiscent of African textiles. His work has been featured in numerous international exhibitions since the early 1970s. His work was part of the 50th Venice Biennale and was included in the Dakar Biennial. Museum exhibitions include those at the National Academy Museum, the Nelson-Atkins Museum of Art, the University of Dayton, the Pennsylvania Academy of Fine Arts, the Alternative Museum in New York. Whitney's work is part of museum and private collections worldwide.

Influential visual artist and political activist, **Fred Wilson** (1954, New York, USA) describes himself as of African, Native American, European and Amerindian descent. In 2012, the Cleveland Museum of Art hosted his solo show: *Works 2004-2011*. Wilson represented the United States at the Cairo Biennial in 1992 and at the Venice Biennale in 2003. His work is represented in numerous important public and private collections.

NERO SU BIANCO

Curated and edited by
Lyle Ashton Harris, Robert Storr
and Peter Benson Miller

With the patronage of the
Embassy of the United States
of America

The exhibition is made possible
by the Syde Hurdus Foundation

Additional support is provided
by Miyoung Lee and Neil Simpkins

The catalogue is made possible
by the DEPART Foundation

AMERICAN ACADEMY IN ROME
President and CEO
Mark Robbins
Director
Kimberly Bowes
Andrew Heiskell Arts Director
Peter Benson Miller
Senior Programs Officer
Anne Coulson
Exhibition Organization
and Coordination
Lexi Eberspacher
Exhibition Assistant
Matteo Ventricelli
Press
Santa Nastro
Gallery Installation
Stefano Silvia
and Andrea Polichetti

Insurance
Arte Assicurazioni Srl
Transport
Apice

Catalogue designed
and published by NERO
Lorenzo Micheli Gigotti,
editing
Francesco de Figueiredo,
art direction
Federico Antonini,
layout
Karen Tomatis,
copy editing and proofreading

Individual orders and information:
distribution@neromagazine.it
www.neromagazine.it

Editorial advisement on the
interview with Frank M. Snowden, III
Tommy Gear

Studio Manager
for Lyle Ashton Harris
Michael Adno

The American Academy in Rome
would like to express its gratitude
to all of the participating artists,
the contributors to the catalogue
and the following lenders:
The Estate of Terry Adkins
APT Institute, New York
Galleria Continua, San Gimignano
– Beijing – Les Moulins
Galleria Raffaella Cortese, Milan
Hiscox Collection, London
Galleria Francesca Minini, Milan
Mauro Nicoletti, Rome
NOMAS Foundation, Rome
Galleria Lorcan O'Neill, Rome
Pace Gallery, New York
Michael Rosenfeld Gallery, New York
Salon 94, New York
Jack Shainman Gallery, New York
Galleria Vistamare, Pescara

Special thanks to:
Anna Abbà, Michael Adno,
Domenico Avella, Douglas
Baxter, Christine Begley, Giorgio
Benni, Giulia Bruno, Francesco
Cagnizzi, Cecilia Canziani, Colutto
Cornici, Tamara Corm, Gregory
Crewdson, Elisa Del Prete, Luigi
De Marco, James Demby, Marie
d'Origny, Barbara Drudi, John
Edmonds, Davide Franceschini,
Elisa Francesconi, Vittorio Gaddi,
Stefano Genna, Elisa Genovesi,
Alexandra Goullier, Lindsay R.
Harris, Whitney Hintz, Jennifer
Hsu, Joseph Imhauser, Irfecolore,
Caroline Jennings, Evelyn Kahsay,
Sarah Kurz, Marina Lella, Debora
Levi, Parissah Lin, Sara Lipton,
Cristina Lombardi-Diop, Costanza
Mazzonis di Pralafera, Brian
McCamley, Marques McClary,
Lindsay McGuire, Darcy Merante,
Gregory R. Miller, Lou Miller, Liz
Moore, Giovanni Panebianco, Pina
Pasquantonio, Amy Pennington,
Alberto Peola, Sarah Poppel,
Cristina Puglisi, Nancy Rattenbury,
Giulia Ravaglioli, Elisa Scaramuzzino,
Stefano and Raffaella Sciarretta,
Anna Serotta, Melanie Sherazi,
Benedetta Spalletti, Justin
Randolph Thompson, Treeitalia,
Alessandra Vinciguerra, Kevin Walz,
Michael Weiner, Merele Williams,
Emanuela Zirzotti.

Photography credits

pg 11	Mimmo Capone
pg 36	John Edmonds
pg 51	altrospazio
pg 59	John White
pg 61	Kerry Ryan McFate
pg 63	© Armin Linke, 2012
pg 65	© Armin Linke, 2012
pg 67	© Armin Linke, 2012
pg 69	© Armin Linke, 2012
pg 73	Krzysztof Zielinski and Theo Eshetu
pg 74-75	Krzysztof Zielinski and Theo Eshetu
pg 80-81	Bridget Baker
pg 83	Bridget Baker
pg 85	Florine Leoni
pg 86	Florine Leoni
pg 110-111	James Wang
pg 126-127	Giorgio Benni
pg 129	Leonardo Petrucci
pg 131	Leonardo Petrucci
pg 132-133	Roberto Marossi
pg 147	Jebila Okongwu
pg 149	altrospazio